ELEPHANTS DON'T BITE

ELEPHANTS DON'T BITE

*How Doing the Little Things
Right Can Make a Big Difference
in Your Career—and Your Life*

by Vernon Crawford

DONALD I. FINE, INC.
New York

Crawford, Vernon.
Elephants don't bite : how doing the little things right can make
a big difference in your career—and your life / Vernon Crawford.
p.   cm.
ISBN 1-55611-240-8
1. Success in business.   2. Business etiquette.   I. Title.
HF5386.C8934   1991
650.1--dc20   90-56064
CIP

Manufactured in the United States of America

Designed by Irving Perkins Associates

10   9   8   7   6   5   4   3   2   1

This book in no way reflects the Joel H. Weldon seminar
or tapes entitled "Elephants Don't Bite."

*Dedicated to Michael LeBoeuf and Maurice Villere
for their helpful suggestions, and to my former boss,
Nick Dimitroff, for making me painfully aware of
the mosquitoes of life*

WITH SPECIAL THANKS TO:

Harriet Handshaw, Tim Keogh, and Alma Dalluge
for their excellent editing. Artie Pine,
my inspirational agent. The members
of the National Speakers Association
and the American Society of Training and Development
for their ideas and encouragement.
Maurice Villere, John Vaughn and Michael LeBoef
for their contributions. Donald I. Fine, Inc.
for publishing my books, and to all the troublesome
mosquitoes that have bitten me.

Contents

CHAPTER SIX: OFFICE DECOR   72

CHAPTER SEVEN: BUSINESS POLITICS   82

CHAPTER EIGHT: COMMUNICATIONS   108

PREFACE

THE ADVENTURES OF PLASTIC MAN

ONCE A LONG-HAIRED hippie, now a corporate executive. How did he make the transition, how did he survive?

Plastic Man: feared by no one, hated by few (at least by no one who really matters). He roams the corporate corridors with his coat buttoned and his wing-tip shoes shined. His face is shaven and his hair is shorn. Now he wears Polo instead of patchouli and a necktie instead of love beads.

What happened to that hippie? Did he sell out to the establishment? Did he change his values? Since he is now over thirty, can he be trusted? Does he trust himself?

This is an autobiographical tale of a flower child and eternal college student. I lived in San Francisco during the summer of love. I had shoulder-length hair, bell-bottom jeans, and a Nehru Jacket. This book is about changing many little personal traits in order to fit into the executive jungle.

I am what industrial psychologists like to call a "late

bloomer." Thirty-two is fairly old to enter the land of the starched shirt. Actually, it was not my choice of destinies.

In 1978 I lived with my "old lady" in a small trailer, near the middle of Honey Island Swamp in Louisiana. We had the good life, teaching a few courses at a local university, raising an organic vegetable garden, and catching an occasional catfish. My mother, the owner of our humble abode, was getting tired of watching her only son "waste his life." She was fond of saying, "After fourteen years of college, is this all you can do?"

Early one morning (9:30) the phone rang. A female voice said into my groggy head, "We have reviewed your resumé and we would like to interview you." I yawned and said, "Ok . . . where and when?" She gave me the name of a company of which I had never heard (even though it was a Fortune 500 company). "We want to see you day after tomorrow at 3:00 P.M." I said, "OK." That was the end of the conversation.

After a few cups of café au lait, I finally woke up to the fact that I was going to interview with an unknown company for an unknown position. I did what I usually do during times of crises: I called my mother.

After I told her of my situation, she started laughing. I yelled, "Mom, I'm in a fix. How can you laugh like that?" She said, "I typed your resumé and a cover letter, forged your signature, and mailed it." With my typical spoiled-brat attitude I said, "I wish you would tell me when you do things like that."

As it turned out the job was for a corporate trainer. Previously I had taught a few seminars, but I still had no idea what a corporate trainer was supposed to do.

That afternoon I went to the library, read about the company and checked out John T. Malloy's *Dress for Success*. I brought the book to a men's haberdasher and with Malloy's help selected a medium-gray suit, a pair of black wing-tip shoes, and had the salesman select a shirt and tie. Then, the suit had to be altered, and would not be ready until 2:00 P.M. on Friday.

I said, "No problem, my interview isn't until 3:00 P.M."

The next day rolled by slowly. I got my hair cut, dug the swamp mud out from under my fingernails and read everything I could find on "training."

At exactly 2:00 P.M. I arrived at the store to put on my new suit. The suit fit and I felt spiffy. This was only the second article of clothing that I had ever bought that cost over $100. The first was a brown suede western jacket with fringe on the front and back.

Feeling confident, I boarded the elevator and punched 30. The ride took forever and I suddenly needed to use the restroom. When I got off the elevator the scene that hit me almost made me soil my pants. The view from thirty stories up was awesome. Honey Island Swamp is six inches below sea level.

The interview went amazingly well... considering that I was winging it. Luckily the interviewer was an avid gardener. Most of our conversation consisted of chit-chat about the best way to grow collard greens. The next day they offered me the job. I promptly accepted. The starting salary was three times more than I had ever made before in a single year.

I was higher than I'd ever been on Haight Street in San Francisco. The job meant a lot to me and I didn't want to screw up. I consulted with my good friend Plastic Man. P.M. is an old college buddy that was mollified by corporate America at the tender age of twenty-three. He told me of some of the ins and outs, but he could not prevent me from being bitten by many mosquitoes during my ten-year corporate career.

This book will warn you of the pitfalls in adjusting to modern corporate America. I've been bitten by most of the mosquitoes, and have observed hundreds of people being eaten alive during interviews that I've conducted, but before I decided to actually write this book, I sat down with a few close friends and kicked around the idea. The all liked the title and offered some mosquitoes that had escaped me. With all of their positive support I went to bed keyed-up and ready to write.

That night I dreamt that I was being interviewed on national television by Maria Schriver. With her azure eyes beaming at me she asked, "I understand you are writing a new book entitled, *Elephants Don't Bite*. Would you explain the title for us?"

I asked Maria, "Have you ever been bitten by an elephant?" She said, "No."

"Have you ever been bitten by a gnat or a mosquito?" She said, "Of course."

"Most of us know how to do the job we were hired to do. The personnel department makes sure of that. After we're hired, it's the little things that bite us and deter our careers."

Maria asked "And you have identified some of these?"

"Yes, I have identified 100 of the most common little things that can bite big chunks out of your career plans."

"Can you give us some examples?"

"In broad categories I have tips on business etiquette, politics, social savvy, communications, physical appearance, office decor, and sex.

Maria held up her hand and said, "We'll have to stop here, I'm afraid we're out of time, the book sounds very interesting, especially the part about sex."

That's when I woke up. I told my wife about the dream and she said, "Did you notice that she has crooked teeth? If these little things are so important, how come she can be so successful and still have crooked teeth?"

I said, "With Maria's azure eyes, professional ability, Kennedy family connection and Arnold Schwarzenegger for a husband, a little thing like crooked teeth may not stand in her way. On the other hand, we don't know how many other opportunities she has missed as a result of this 'little thing.'"

My wife said, "I still don't like you dreaming about Maria Schriver."

ELEPHANTS DON'T BITE

INTRODUCTION

HAVE YOUR EVER been bitten by a mosquito, bothered by a gnat or stung by a bee? Almost everyone will respond "Yes" to at least one of these questions. On the other hand, how many of us have ever been bitten by an elephant? Few, if any, will respond affirmatively to this question. The point is: it's most often the little things—the mosquitoes—that make the difference between success and failure in our lives and our careers. Everyone is trying to accomplish big things, not realizing that life is composed of many little things.

Most often, it's the little things that count, things such as office decor...lunch etiquette...knowing when to call or when to write...courtesy on the elevator...punctuality... wardrobe savvy...tactful handling of touchy customers, and proper telephone tactics.

Often, the difference between a seat in the executive suite or one on a much lower level has little to do with our technical or decision-making skills. The difference often lies in our ability to deal with the swarms of "mosquitoes" we encounter every day.

1

Most of us know at least a few very hard-working, dedicated employees who seem to do more than their fair share—but never seem to get ahead. Perhaps we count ourselves among this unfortunate group, as we wonder why Bill, Jane, and Bob get all the promotions and raises and we don't. Why does Mary Lou get invited to all the best parties while we sit at home? How is it that Terry's career has taken off like a rocket, while ours plods along at a snail's pace?

When we reflect on these unhappy comparisons, we realize that our associates are not working any harder or more diligently, nor do they seem to make better decisions or close more deals. So we're left wondering: What is the difference? What is the secret of their greater success?

Years of corporate observation, personal experience and private reflection have convinced me that in the end, it's the little things (the mosquitoes) and not the big things (the elephants) that generally tip the balance toward success.

For example:

- A salesperson may know her product and may make an excellent sales presentation, but if she argues with the customer she can forget about the sale.
- A young executive may impress the boss with his initiative and insight on an important project, but if he speaks out of turn at a planning meeting, his efforts will go for naught.
- An ambitious attorney may craft the best legal arguments around, but her chances of winning a case in court may be slim if she dresses like a modern-day Moll Flanders.
- A personnel assistant may develop an expertly designed policy manual; only to have it shot down from above because of numerous editing errors.
- The head of research and development may invite the rising new staff member to lunch, but quickly become

disenchanted when she is rude to the waiter, and exhibits poor table manners.

The previous examples have a common, very crucial theme: in every case, the quality of the employee's work effort may have been excellent, but unfortunately, little things—or mosquitoes—prevented career success. The purpose of this book is to lead you on an exploration of these little things.

CHAPTER ONE—WHY LITTLE THINGS COUNT

The opening chapter explains why little things count, and the importance of recognizing and adequately dealing with troublesome mosquitoes in everyday life. Answers are provided to questions such as: Why do we have particular rules of conduct? Why do we dress the way we do? Who says *this* is proper—and *that* is not? What world events have helped create our current value systems?

To demonstrate how value systems develop, a brief history of major events in America from 1930–1990 is given. Topics such as styles of dress, attitudes toward work, and policy formation are examined on a generational basis and projected into the year 2000. Perhaps most importantly, you will learn why many people still love Elvis.

CHAPTER TWO—ETIQUETTE

This chapter provides the basics of good business manners, everything from eating to elevator etiquette. This chapter helps the reader avoid social blunders during the all-important interview, and in situations commonly encountered once the job is won.

CHAPTER THREE—DRESSING FOR BUSINESS

How we dress often determines how we are treated, both socially and professionally. If we dress in an overly casual or careless fashion, we risk being treated as if we're unimportant or as someone who does not take his or her job seriously. Also, how we dress affects how fully we are accepted within an organization.

Unlike some blue-collar workers and first-line service personnel, white-collar workers invariably choose their own working wardrobes. As a result, we may choose a shirt style or color that is inconsistent with company culture. Some organizations prefer the Ivy League or the button-down look, while others may think such a look is too preppie or juvenile. Some companies may limit color choice to white or blue; others may be so daring as to permit pinstriped designs.

Some employers frown on women who wear pants, short skirts or spiked heels. Conservative companies may strongly prefer black wing-tip shoes for men and low-heeled pumps for women.

Unless they are currently in style, suit lapels as wide as Dumbo's ears are a cause for executive embarrassment.

CHAPTER FOUR—SOCIAL SAVVY

Knowing how to relate to others on a social level has considerable impact on one's job success. In lieu of a complete guide to business manners, often a few key tips about little social things, or mosquitoes, can make the difference between looking like a klutz and looking like Miss Manners. For example, knowing how to shake hands with a peer or new customer can help start a positive relationship and develop rapport. A wimpy or a vise-like handshake will not do. Who initiates the hand-shake? What kind of eye contact should be made?

CHAPTER FIVE—PHYSICAL APPEARANCE

Like it or not, how we look to others profoundly affects our professional and social success. Suggestions are offered on losing or hiding unwanted pounds, quitting smoking or at least hiding the fact that you smoke, and developing better posture. Rather than subject the reader to a weighty sermon, this chapter examines social attitudes toward the overweight, smokers, and other detriments to success.

CHAPTER SIX—OFFICE DECOR

In this chapter, you will learn how to arrange office furniture for maximum communication, how to choose an appropriate backdrop, and how to create a more compassionate image. The reader will be encouraged to examine and assess every aspect of office decor for visitor impact.

Many of us have no use for computers. Some of us have computerphobia. Nevertheless, computers as office decor are here for the nineties. The reader will be treated to an exploration into the value of the computer as a paper weight.

CHAPTER SEVEN—BUSINESS POLITICS

Business is a political party where everyone is a candidate and everyone must run his or her own campaign. Like a politician, workers are expected to go to company parties, shake every-one's hand, kiss the babies, and smile.

This chapter explores how to avoid the most dangerous

enemy in the business world... the political enemy. Careers are made and destroyed on the political battlefield. The reader is offered a battle plan for avoiding the hidden booby-traps that lurk in corporate corridors.

CHAPTER EIGHT—COMMUNICATIONS

One of the most common complaints of business executives is that employees do not know how to communicate effectively. It is estimated that tens of billions of dollars are lost each year due to poor or improper communications skills. Poor productivity, low morale, and a lack of cooperation among staff members are usually related to communication problems. This chapter addresses a number of mosquitoes and will help pave the way to more effective business communications. One point involves the issue of knowing when to write and when to speak. Other topics include nonverbal skills and suggestions on how to listen for better understanding. Still other topics deal with cross-cultural communications and how to use the telephone to your best advantage.

CHAPTER NINE—PERSONALITY

The purpose of this chapter is not to introduce therapeutic techniques designed to correct major personality problems. It does contain behavioral mosquitoes that may interfere with your success at the office and suggest some ways of dealing with them. You will learn how to conduct yourself during the so-called "confidential chat" with the company shrink, and why it is more important to appear nice than it is to give off an air of importance.

CHAPTER TEN—HOW TO GET CONTROL OF THE LITTLE THINGS

This chapter offers nine practical suggestions on how to handle the "little things" that can drive you batty. If you follow the suggestions in this chapter you will not only handle mosquitoes with ease, you will also live longer, relax more, stay healthier, and have greater enjoyment in work and life.

LESSONS MY FATHER TAUGHT ME

When I was about eight or nine, I was supposed to meet my father about an hour before sundown at this gigantic sycamore tree in Honey Island Swamp. We were going to set out some catfish lines; it's difficult to set out lines by yourself. The tree was big so we used it as a landmark. After school, I set out to meet my father. I walked into the swamp and looked up in the sky for the old sycamore that would guide me to my father. To my astonishment there was no tree, only empty sky. In a panic I searched for my father, and by the time I found him the sun was going down. In the Louisiana swamp, when the sun goes down, swarms of mosquitoes and gnats come out. They were eating me alive and I knew that the bugs would find my father just as tasty. The mosquitoes were enough to drive a saint insane. I was sorry I had let my father down and afraid he would be mad at me. As I approached him he smiled.

The gigantic sycamore that I had played in and used as a landmark was toppled. I asked my Dad what happened. He said, "Son, this tree had stood for some four hundred years. It was half grown when the Pilgrims settled at Plymouth and not yet fully grown when the French Canadians settled in Louisiana. During the course of its long life it was struck by lightning twenty-two times and endured innumerable hurricanes. It survived them all. In the end, however, an army of beetles attacked the tree and leveled it to the ground. The insects ate their way through the bark and gradually destroyed the inner strength of the tree by their repeated attacks. This old giant sycamore tree that had endured lighting and hurricanes fell at last before beetles so small that a man could crush them between his forefinger and thumb." It was amazing that something so great, so strong, could be toppled by such little things as those tiny beetles.

I learned an important lesson that day, a lesson that I've relearned again and again, as I watched employees who are essentially good and strong toppled—or kept from growing—by little things; things as insignificant as mosquitoes that they could have learned to avoid.

CHAPTER ONE

WHY LITTLE THINGS COUNT

Trifles make up the happiness or the misery of human life.

—ALEXANDER SMITH

LIKE THE OLD sycamore tree, we often survive the major problems in life and then let the little things get us down. Coping with the little things and doing little things right can make a big difference in your career and life. Life is not one big event, but rather a series of small events. The events are further broken down into individual actions. Individual actions are created by our thoughts. What we think and feel is determined by our value systems.

9

VALUE SYSTEM FORMATION

> *Every man is a creature of the age in which he lives;*
> *very few are able to raise themselves above the ideas*
> *of their times.*
>
> —VOLTAIRE

Our value system formation begins at a very early age; some say at the moment of birth. Some parents chose to have a warm, dimly lit room with homey surroundings for the birthing room as opposed to a brightly lit hospital clinic. At birth the baby is placed in warm water to simulate the womb. These parents feel that the impressions etched on the blank value system slate of the newly born make a lasting impression.

Most people agree that early childhood experiences play a major role in the values we have as adults—experiences such as the lessons we were taught in school, the television programs we watched, the church we attended, our friends, relatives, and parents, and everything else that had an impact on us. By the time we reach the age of ten our values are well formed. Only a major social event will change those values.

In order to understand the value systems of the leaders of corporate America and the heads of state we must examine *when* their value systems were formed.

OLDIES BUT GOODIES

Most of the world's leaders were value-programmed during the Great Depression of the 1930s. Theirs was a society of strong families, in which women stayed home and the family gathered around the dinner table every night. Children were either taught manners or they learned them by example. They grew up knowing how to behave and often don't understand people who don't know how to behave. Jobs were scarce and when you had a job it was highly valued. These are the people who say, "When I was your age I had to walk five miles in the snow to get to school."

Our laws, policies, procedures, and rules of conduct are made by the people who sign our paychecks. Their value systems are dominated by the need for security. This need becomes ever more apparent as we see a military build-up so high that we could blow up the world three times over, and golden parachutes so rich that the foundations of their companies will shake when they collect.

Twenty years ago I had to use a company-issued form when interviewing prospective employees. One of the questions on the form was "Does he look like one of us?" This question was made illegal through the efforts of the baby boomers protesting for equal rights during the 1960s. There are equal opportunity laws, but this doesn't mean you should disguise yourself as a handicapped black woman. The law forbids discrimination, but you can't legislate values. The attitude of "If he doesn't look like one of us, then he must be one of them, and we don't trust them," still prevails. Today, our aging leaders live in a rapidly changing world and often encounter social situations for which the etiquette has changed.

The generation value-programmed in the 1940s has now become our upper-level management. The major event in their value-programming years was World War II. Patriotism reigned supreme. Loyalty to spouse, country, and place of employment rank high on their list of values.

BABY BOOMERS

Then came the baby boomers, value-programmed in the 1950s. Most of the workers in America today fit into this category. Much to the chagrin of the two previous generations the values of the baby boomers were different. This was an era of prosperity and permissiveness. They experienced several simultaneous social revolutions such as rock & roll, rebellion against authority, and civil and women's rights. Communication between parents and teenagers withered. The establishment was denigrated and the subject of manners was considered "uncool" by anyone over the age of thirteen. The disloyalty during the Vietnam War, long hair, and the "Bon Temps Roule" attitude left our leaders feeling like failed parents.

CEOs want the values of their employees to be the same as theirs: work is hard and serious, and nonconformity is frowned upon. Work is not peace, love, and "do your own thing."

To thrive in corporate America today the baby boomers of the world must adapt. Outward attitudes must soften and the hair must go. Most CEOs are antihair. They want it short, the shorter the better. This attitude was first developed during World War I. Only one size helmet was made and it was easier to fit everyone if they all had short hair. Besides, it's hard to aim at and shoot someone with hair hanging in your eyes. Short hair is easier to wash and by making everyone have short hair the need for military conformity was satisfied. The value was set: the heroes had short hair and those who did not defend their country had long hair.

Remember when Elvis was drafted and his haircut made national news? Young girls wept while the older generation applauded. For the oldsters, Elvis had moved up from being a hip swinging punk to being one of "our boys." Unlike many performers, Elvis endeared himself across several generations and his posthumous popularity attests to that today.

Facial hair is a symbol of antiestablishment freedom. Goatees are definitely unacceptable, possibly because they look too satanic, and handlebar mustaches are thought to indicate a large ego. A full but well-trimmed beard is somewhat more acceptable on a junior executive, but not on a company officer.

The bottom line is: the less hair you are comfortable with, the better the corporate leaders will like you.

YUPPIES

Every generation revolts against its fathers and makes friends with its grandfathers.

—LEWIS MUMFORD

The generation value-programmed in the 1970s (yuppies) has many of the ideals of yesteryear. They want "things" and they are willing to put in the office hours to get them. They have an easier time adjusting to life as it is today than did their parents. It's like we have gone full circle. The one major value that is different is company loyalty. Yuppies were influenced by the dishonesty of Watergate, the antiheroes of the media and multimarriages. The mosquitoes of the "Me Generation" are: a low level of manners awareness, a lack of loyalty and a selfish attitude. They often commit faux pas but are unaware of the blunder. John D. Rockefeller said, "The ability to get along with people is as purchasable as sugar and coffee, and I pay more for that ability than any under the sun." With the advent of the "Me Decade," however, top management began to lament the difficulty of finding outstanding people handlers. One executive said, "Being able to work with others is the single most important characteristic a junior executive can have. I can always buy specialized knowledge, but being able to work with others is a rare commodity." Good manners are essential in building good relationships.

Manners make the fortune of ambitious youth.

—EMERSON

Manners must be learned, loyalty must be established and their selfish attitude must be disguised or tempered if they are to jive with the oldies.

> INTERVIEWER: From your references I see you've worked in four different places within the last year.
> YUPPIE: Yes, sir, but that shows how much in demand I am.

Loyalty is a form of trust. Yuppies often do not realize the importance most companies place on it. They will trade off loyalty for a gain that is too small or a goal that is too short-sighted. An executive once said to me, "An extra nickel in their paycheck will buy you a yuppie."

The older generation and the yuppies have a work ethic that is very strong. An older gentleman once told the author about his efforts in looking for work when he was a much younger man. He said he refused a job working in a factory twelve hours a day, six days a week because he didn't want part-time work.

THE VALUE OF VALUES

The success of a society depends on its values. The decline of the Roman Empire is attributed to a fracture in their value system. America was founded on the Protestant work ethic, an honest, hard-working, uncomplaining soul, loyal and obedient to the company and God, preferably in that order. With this ethic as a foundation and with only 5 percent of the world's population, the United States produces one fourth of the world's gross national product—more than Japan and the Soviet Union *combined.*

Webster's defines a psychopathic personality as, "an emotionally and behaviorally disordered state characterized by clear perception of reality except for the individual's social and moral obligations and often by the pursuit of immediate personal gratifications in criminal acts, drug addiction, or sexual perversion." The Roman Emperor Nero may have been psychopathic: he killed his mother, his brother, two of his wives, and his philosophy teacher. When a great fire destroyed almost all of Rome, rumors were spread that Nero started it. Nero shifted the blame from himself to the Christians. Under Nero the scapegoat Christians were executed.

Without value systems not only do individuals suffer, entire civilizations and organizations can crumble. Manners are the basis of good human relationships. They govern how people treat each other. When people who work together adhere to the rules of social behavior, their workplace becomes more efficient and effective. When an individual's values are not trusted by his or her employer, there is little the individual can do, except resign. Your honesty should be beyond reproach: never bring home office supplies, hedge on expense accounts, or make long-distance calls on the company's nickel.

The boss approached his office manager and told him, "There's $100 missing from the safe, and you and I are the only ones who have the keys to it. So what have you to say?" The office manager said, "Well, why don't we each put up $50 and forget about it?"

Every organization—in business, education, and politics—has its own values, tempo, atmosphere, culture and way of doing things. Be sure you understand the values and way of life of your company.

VALUES IN THE YEAR 2000

Between the year 2000 and 2010 the entire demographic structure of leadership will shift to the baby boomers. Their value systems will determine policies, laws, and corporate cultures. As a result we will see a major restructuring of employee and employer relationships. Henry Ford once said, "Nobody can really guarantee the future. The best we can do is size up the chances, calculate the risks involved, estimate our ability to deal with them, and make our plans with confidence."

Some of the changes we can expect to see are:

- Flexible working hours
- More company-sponsored day care and exercise facilities
- A shift from bossing subordinates to counseling valued team members
- More equality for women and minorities in pay and pro-motions
- A shift from centralization to decentralization (do your own thing)
- A loosening in dress code expectations
- Increased company-sponsored "socializing"

As John Naisbitt and Patricia Aburdene say in *Megatrends 2000,* "The most exciting breakthroughs of the twenty-first century will occur not because of technology but because of an expanding concept of what it means to be human."

ELEPHANTS DON'T CHANGE

An important thing to remember about values is that values are a set of beliefs that have no basis in fact. No one can prove, for example, that racism, communism, democracy, religion or any other belief is either good or bad. All of these values are true within our own value system program.

Education after the formative years has little effect on our values. In Africa, baby elephants are chained to a stake so they can't go beyond the length of the chain. When fully grown the elephant can be restrained by a string and a small spike.

If a tiger attacks the elephant, it will break the string to get away. We too are tied to a spike by our value systems, and only through a major event, like a symbolic tiger attack, can we break loose from our value programming.

Our values allow us to have an opinion on everything, regardless of how little we may know about it. On virtually any subject, we can create an opinion from our never-ending flow of value system responses. People expressing ideas contrary to our beliefs are wrong; our belief is the only right belief. We don't like to listen to someone with opposing beliefs. Most of the time we act like the old man who would turn his hearing aid off when his wife was nagging him.

Some people try to convert others to their beliefs; political propagandists, and recently saved crusaders are the most adamant. These protagonists rarely succeed unless there is some type of value programming from the past supporting the beliefs being thrust upon the nonbeliever.

Changing values through reason and logic is usually futile. Logic and reason are conscious processes, while value programming is largely absorbed subconsiously. When trying to make someone believe something different from his or her original programming, you are shaking the very foundation of that person's subconscious mind.

When it comes to changing values, we would rather fight than switch. Indeed, many religious and political wars down through the ages have been fought because of a differing of values, rather than imperial aggression. When faced with undeniable logic that is contrary to our beliefs, we will either rationalize around it, not listen, or become belligerent. None of these responses do we want to elicit from our employer.

CHAPTER TWO

ETIQUETTE

ETIQUETTE IS TO business what oil is to machinery. It costs nothing, yet it buys things that are priceless. Webster's defines etiquette as: "The forms required by good breeding or prescribed by authority to be observed in social or official life." When one knows the proper form, one can more easily move through the world with grace and ease. The information that follows is only a fragment of etiquette standards. Learning the rules of proper conduct is a lifetime process. What follows are a few of the more worrisome mosquitoes.

THE BUSINESS LUNCH

There are many deals cut while slicing your veal during a business lunch. Neither underestimate the value of sitting down over a meal to hammer out a business deal nor underestimate the devastating effects of the inability to handle that meal. The business lunch has become so important that one eastern business school requires their MBA candidates to take

18

a two-semester, three-credit course called, "The Dynamics and Management of the Business Lunch."

There are two purposes for a business lunch. The first is purely social. Its purpose is to strengthen informal business bonds, woo a client, or aid in team building. The second is the working lunch, at which the participants agree to discuss business. This type of lunch may even have a typed agenda.

Business lunches are also used to woo an unhappy executive, celebrate a promotion, and to evaluate a prospective employee.

A well-qualified candidate for an important, decision-making position was turned down because the interviewer felt that the candidate did not think before making a decision. Everyone else who had interviewed the candidate was very impressed.

The interviewer had taken the candidate to lunch at an exclusive restaurant. When the food arrived, the candidate liberally sprinkled his food with salt. Being health conscious, the interviewer was unimpressed and concluded the candidate did not think before making decisions. The moral is: taste before you shake.

When invited to lunch during the interview process, good manners are essential. To make the lunch a success:

- Order items that can be eaten easily. No one wants to spend the rest of the day with reminders of spaghetti on a tie or blouse.
- Watch the booze. Samuel Johnson said, "One of the disadvantages of wine is that it makes a man mistake words for thoughts."
- Small talk should not get into ethical, religious or political subjects, unless you know the preferences of your interviewer. An interviewer once told an interviewee that the company may open an office in a really nice place— Green Bay, Wisconsin. The interviewee said, "What's

nice about it? The only things ever to come out of Green Bay are football players and ugly girls." The interviewer got angry and said, "Wait a second—my wife is from Green Bay!" The interviewee said, "Oh? What position does she play?"

• Safe subjects are the weather, sports, common interests, and common acquaintances. Samuel Johnson said, "That is the happiest conversation where there is no competition, no vanity, but a calm quiet interchange of sentiments."

The business lunch is where all of your social skills and graces come together. Your table manners, ability to speak well, and your ability to handle others can be evaluated during the business lunch. Many centuries ago, a Japanese man could be executed for using poor table manners. Don't let poor table manners prevent you from getting that job, wooing that client or impressing a potential significant other.

The trend toward fitness has influenced the business lunch. People are eating fewer desserts, ordering more seafood and drinking less hard liquor. To wash down their broiled sole, executives are drinking white wine, iced tea or sparkling water with a twist. There is also a trend toward the forty-five-minute lunch. The good old days of the two-hour, three-martini lunch are rapidly going the way of their consumers... down Boot Hill.

HOW TO GET FOOD FROM YOUR PLATE AND INTO YOUR MOUTH

> *Put not another bit into your mouth till the*
> *former is Swallowed.*
> *Cleanse not your teeth with the Table Cloth,*
> *Napkin, or Fork or Knife.*

Spit not into the fire.
Kill no Vermin as Flees, lice, ticks & ect. in the
Sight of Others.

—GEORGE WASHINGTON (age fifteen)
Rules of Civility

Business executives who have already made it to the top frequently lament the lack of social polish in their employees. One of the first places rough edges show up is at the table. It is not simply that no one wants to eat with a slob. The lack of table manners is an indication of the level of your sophistication. Good manners at the dinner table are something every parent tries to teach his or her child. Why are good manners so hard? Because we are hungry: we want to get some food into our stomachs. We take big bites, chew as little as possible, and swallow, paying little attention to the mess we are making on the table. We must learn to eat slowly. As Emerson said, "Manners require time, as nothing is more vulgar than haste."

Some basic table manners (that your mother should have taught you) follow:

- Don't begin to eat until everyone has been served.
- Don't slouch in your seat or rock back in your chair.
- Don't chew with your mouth open.
- Don't eat and talk at the same time.
- Take small bites.
- Don't mash or mix your food, i.e., don't mix your peas with your mashed potatoes.
- Break your bread rather than cut it with a knife.
- Don't blow on hot food or drink to cool it.
- Don't sip coffee from your saucer or spoon.
- Don't tuck your napkin under the collar of your shirt or use the napkin to wipe off cutlery or to blow your nose. Simply place it on your lap.
- Always ask for food to be passed to you unless it is directly in front of you.

- Keep your elbows off the table.
- When eating, do not move your entire arm. Use a simple wrist movement and move your arm as little as possible.
- Never use your thumb to push food onto your fork or spoon.
- If you're in the South you may eat finger foods with your fingers.
- In the North use a knife and fork for finger foods.
- After eating don't start picking your teeth with your toothpick or, worst yet, your fingernails. Go to the restroom to do that.
- After eating don't push your plate away, loosen your belt, and belch.

A middle-aged female executive has a vivid memory of Texas courtesy: She was struggling with a hot cup of coffee in a small-town railway station, trying to gulp it before the train pulled out. A cowboy, seated a couple of stools away, noted her plight. Seeing the guard waving to the woman, he came to her rescue. "Here ma'am, you can take my cup of coffee. It's already saucered and blowed."

In summary, good table manners are simple: eat slowly, take a small bite, chew thoroughly, then swallow, and try not to make a mess. Use your napkin and don't take more than your share of the wine.

DINING DIFFERENCES

When dining in a different country, you will come across many customs and cuisines radically different from our own. Acceptance of what is on your plate is synonymous with acceptance of the host, country, and company. Some dishes may make you want to gag, but you must eat them anyway . . . anyway you can.

During a visit to Singapore I was given an honorary dinner. The dish for such occasions, I was told, was fish head curry.

I was seated at the head of the table with a dozen Singaporians impatiently awaiting this local delicacy. The waiter appeared with an enormous red fish head, no tail, just the head. The dish was placed before me. The waiter, using a special spoon, scooped out the eyeball and placed it on my plate. Everyone was quiet and had a look of expectation on their faces. It became obvious that I was expected to eat this eyeball before the meal began. I was repulsed, but I didn't want to offend anyone. Assuming that the eyeball was mainly fluid, I hesitatingly spooned the eyeball into my mouth. My plan was to pop the eyeball and quickly gulp it down and the chase it with a beer. No such luck. The eyeball had a gristly texture that had to be chewed. As I chewed, it seemed to grow in my mouth rather than diminish. I managed to swallow the eyeball, everyone smiled and the meal began. Incidentally, the rest of the meal was delicious.

Being a world business traveler, I have eaten many things that I would not have chosen from a menu: monkey brains in Malaysia, bear's paw and shark fin soup in China, live wine shrimp in Singapore and live fish in Japan. No matter what your host puts on your plate, it is impolite not to eat it. The squeamishness comes not so much from the thing itself as from your unfamiliarity with it. After all, an oyster has about the same taste and texture as a fish eyeball.

Another tactic is to not ask what you are eating, just follow the lead of your host. Your host will be flattered and, who knows, maybe it really is chicken in your stew.

THE LONESOME LUNCH

Always mind your manners and try to eat with someone else. Lunch is a great time for networking, learning something about the company, and making friends. Eating with a peer is best, but anybody is better than nobody. If you can't find anyone, order in. Anyone sitting alone in a crowded restaurant looks pathetic and lonely, no matter how hard they try to hide behind their newspapers. If you are alone and want to meet someone of the opposite sex, find someone eating alone and say, "Excuse me, but I hate to eat alone, do you mind if I join you?" Most of the time they will hate eating alone also.

WHO PAYS?

The host, male or female, always pays for the lunch. When you are the host it is your responsibility to ask for the check. Before doing this make sure the meal (and your business) is finished. The person who asks for the check is the person who gets it. When you get the bill, look over it quickly and carefully figure out the tip, and place and your credit card (or money if you must) on the tray, with the check turned face down. In a business lunch, 15 percent is the usual tip.

THE UPS AND DOWNS OF ELEVATOR ETIQUETTE

An elevator can be much more than just a simple conveyance for our bodies. It can also cause our careers to ascend or descend. If you work in a multistoried office building, the only time you may see some fellow employees is on the elevator. No matter how you perform in your office, the impression these coworkers will have of you will be created by your elevator conduct.

THE RULES OF ELEVATOR CONDUCT

- Never press the elevator button more than once. Once pressed and the light comes on, repeated pressings do no good. The elevator doesn't hurry up because you repeatedly press the button.

This behavior probably originated in the 1940s when elevator operators were common. A buzzer sounded in the elevator to alert the operator that you were waiting. Repeated buzzes alerted the operator that you were in a hurry.

Today, repeated button pressing tells other waiting passengers that you are tense, impatient, and that you don't understand simple elevator mechanics. Some may think that you are prone to irrational behavior when under pressure.

- Do not stand in front of the doors while waiting for the elevator. Otherwise, when the elevator arrives, departing passengers must push their way around you to depart. Stand to the side and allow passengers to exit in peace.
- Everyone at the front of a crowded elevator should get off when the doors open. The people in the back can then emerge with ease. If everyone on the elevator is going to get off on the same floor, the people in front should quickly step off and to the side, again to make it easier for those in back.
- It is best to say nothing on an elevator, simply stand there and look up at the floor indicator numbers: if you must talk, be careful about what you say. Rumors and misinformation can be easily started. Two workers may be talking about a layoff in another company. Part of the conversation may be overheard by a fellow passenger and misinterpreted to mean that your company is having a layoff. This information gets grapevined all the way to Wall Street. Immediately your company stock drops thirty points and the stock you've been accumulating for all those years becomes greatly reduced in value.
- Press the hold button when you see someone coming to catch the elevator. It is irritating to have doors close in

your face. Don't forget to say "Thank you" when someone holds the elevator doors for you.

- Stand facing the doors while riding the elevator. A consulting psychologist liked to stand facing the opposite direction so he could observe elevator behavior. He did this while a company officer was on board. The officer felt that this behavior was "too weird." The consultant was never hired by that company again.

- Stand to the back of the elevator when going to the upper floors. If you stand to the front, others have to push around you to get off on the lower floors.

- Some men allow women to get on the elevator first, and to also exit first. In business terms this means FIFO— first in first out. In the Old South this behavior is still expected, especially by older southern women. Other women may become incensed by this intended courtesy. The elevator is not the proper forum to express liberation. The suggested conduct is to quietly get on the elevator. Saying "Thank you," is not necessary.

- Always allow very short people to stand in the front of the elevator. As Buddy Ups said, "A crowded elevator smells different to a short person."

A vice president of a large organization used the elevator to enhance his leadership. He was renowned for his ability to remember everyone's name. In a corporate office building of six hundred employees, he knew everyone's name, their spouse's name, and usually the names and ages of their children. Personnel regularly supplied him with updated employee information, including a photograph of the employee.

When he boarded an elevator he said hello to every employee by name. Many times he would enquire about their children's progress in school, and other personal pleasantries.

Some vice presidents could not get employees to follow them to the restroom after drinking a six-pack of beer. This vice president had a following more loyal than a cub scout troop.

An elevator operator in an exclusive area of San Francisco observed two psychologists who rode his elevator every morning. Each day, one of the psychologists would slap the other's face, while the victim did nothing in return. Finally, the operator stopped the victim after the other exited. "Excuse me sir, but for two years now, I've been taking you and that other man to your respective floors, and each day he slaps your face. Why don't you do something about it? "Well" the psychologist replied with a shrug, "It's *his* problem."

OPENING DOORS

Many of us were taught that women should go through the door first. In some places women still expect this behavior. Others simply acquiesce and allow the man to open the door in the name of getting ahead with the least amount of disturbance, while others feel they are sacrificing their principles. If you are among the latter, you can either politely tell your male colleague that you don't appreciate the chivalry or just beat him to the door next time. Either way, he should get the hint. As Albert Guerard said, "Chivalry is the most delicate form of contempt."

In most places today, however, common sense and efficiency dictate that whoever arrives at the door first should hold it open for those behind and hold it open until all have passed through.

An exception to this rule is that younger executives should open the door for senior executives. When approaching a door with a senior executive, the younger executive should quickly get to the door and hold it open.

Another exception is when an executive is the host for

people who do not work for the company. The host is expected to open doors for his or her guest.

Appropriately opening doors for the right people may incline them to open a career door for you.

BUSINESS CARDS—DON'T LEAVE HOME WITHOUT THEM

On your card include your name, title, your company's name, telephone number, fax number, and address. If you are going where English is not widely spoken, take your cards to that country and have the reverse side printed in the local language.

When overseas, cards are exchanged more frequently than in the United States. They represent proof that you and your company really exist. Many times even a casual acquaintance will ask for your card. Because your name is foreign, it is sometimes easier to comprehend in writing.

Business cards should be clean and of good quality. They should not be offered at the beginning of a conversation. Near or at the end of a conversation is more appropriate. Don't distribute your cards as if they were fliers at a supermarket opening, give them only when asked. Ask for a business card when you are sincere about wanting to remember the person and the company, for whatever reason. Use your card when forwarding material or a resumé to someone.

When introducing yourself by mail, always clip your card to the upper left-hand corner of your letter, so the person receiving it will have a convenient record of you. Most executives do not keep letters on their desk, but a business card can be inserted into a Rolodex.

Always include the loftiest title your profession will allow. A reporter may use Journalist, a secretary may use Administrative Assistant, a janitor may use Sanitation Engineer, and a dishwasher may use Underwater Ceramics Engineer.

THANK-YOU CARDS

Sending thank-you cards is very important. They should be sent when you have received a gift, a favor or special entertainment. Write a personalized note on the inside and sign it with your full name and company name.

A thank-you card is not necessary for business lunches. The thank-you card is a tasteful way to express gratitude. It is also a way to let the gift-giver know that his or her gift has been received and appreciated.

To summarize: etiquette is a way to express kindness and consideration. Either that or etiquette is a way to gracefully manipulate other people without them knowing it. Anyway, etiquette is what your mother always wanted you to have. Whether your mother is Mother Teresa or a scheming manipulator is something that must be decided by you.

CHAPTER THREE

DRESSING FOR BUSINESS

Costly thy habit as they purse can buy,
But not express'd in fancy; rich, not gaudy,
For the apparel oft proclaims the man.
                                   —WILLIAM SHAKESPEARE

MAKING JUDGMENTS AND assessments based on the way one dresses is not peculiar to American culture. Ever since the day Adam felt he needed to clothe himself in a fig leaf, clothing has been an important status symbol. All societies, ancient and modern, have developed some system of measuring and evaluating status among their members. An individual's place in the hierarchy is often determined by the clothes he or she wears. Clothing denotes class and reveals quite a lot about the money and power one possesses. It is a way of showing that one belongs, that one fits in, and that one is a team player.

30

Some criticize conformity of dress, but there is one thing that can be said in favor of it—you can practice it without making a fool of yourself. Few people have the freedom to dress the way they want in the office and still be successful. Even the most rebellious people will find sooner or later that they have to dress like other people at some point in their careers. These people should wear what they want whenever they can, and make it clear that they will dress appropriately when the occasion demands it.

Two and a half centuries ago Confucius said:

> A gentleman does not wear facing of purple or mauve, nor in undress does he use pink or roan. In hot weather he wears an unlined gown of fine thread loosely woven, but puts on an outside garment before going out-of-doors. With a black robe, he wears black lambskin. With a yellow robe, fox fur. On his undress robe the fur cuffs are long; but the right is shorter than the left. His bedclothes must be half as long as his height. The thicker kinds of fox and badger are for home wear. Except when in mourning, he wears all his girdle-ornaments. Apart from his court apron, all his skirts are wider at the bottom than at the waist. Lambskin dyed black and a hat of dark silk must not be worn when making visits of condolence. At the announcement of the new moon, he must go to Court in full Court dress.

Modern-day Saudi Arabians signal their wealth and importance by wearing as much jewelry as they can. Elaborate scarifications on the backs of young men from New Guinea are visible signs of their passage into manhood. In Burma and Thailand the wives of wealthy men allow their necks to be stretched by multiple gold bands. Their necks become so elongated that if the bands are removed the neck could not support the head and would break. Threatening to remove the rings is a form of coercion the men use to control their wives.

Every society has a way of determining rank. Some of these ways are not obvious at first glance. Only with astute observation can one unravel the mysteries of the clothing hierarchy. In any company, clothing is very much a part of your job, and if you delude yourself into thinking that people don't notice, then you are hurting yourself. There is an unwritten code in each company about whether we should shed suit jackets, loosen ties, and roll up sleeves. You have to unravel for yourself whether any or all of these actions are appropriate. Clothing is a statement communicated to the world. Generally, if you do any or all of these things, it is appropriate to unroll your shirt sleeves, put on your jacket, and tighten your tie when you leave your office. The rule for clothing is identical with that for speech: appropriateness!

As Mark Twain so aptly said, "Clothes make the man. Naked people have little or no influence over society."

THE COMPANY SHIRT

When a man is once in fashion, all he does is right.
—LORD CHESTERFIELD

Every organization has a company shirt. At service stations this is sometimes quite obvious: the shirts are issued by the company. When the company does not issue shirts and we can choose our own, we may choose a style or color not in keeping with the company culture.

Some companies are Ivy League, preferring the button-down collar. They were first introduced to America in the early 1900s and have become the mainstay for many businessmen. Other companies consider the buttoned-down look as juvenile or preppie. At these companies straight collars are preferred. The straight collar gives a more formal look, especially when accompanied by French cuffs. Most companies limit color choice to white, pale blue, or for the daring, a subdued blue or red pinstripe. A less conservative company may tolerate white collars and cuffs on solid-colored shirts, even ecru and pink may be worn. Some industries such as advertising, the arts and entertainment will accept most any color.

Many companies frown on women wearing miniskirts or pants. Women seemingly have a little more latitude in their choices of styles and colors. Don't take advantage of this deceptive liberalism; a neck line that's a little too low, a skirt a little too high, or a dress that is too floral can have a more devastating effect than a man wearing the wrong shirt.

TIES THAT BIND

The single most vital piece of apparel is the necktie. Executives notice your tie before sizing up your suit, shirt, or shoes. A high quality tie is worth the investment.

A tie should come to the tip of your belt. Most ties are fifty-five to fifty-six inches long; expensive ties tend to be a little longer. If you are short or very tall, you may have to order custom-made ties. One way around this for the short man is to use a double Windsor knot. This makes a larger knot than the more current half Windsor and takes up more tie length.

Ties should be made of silk or a silk and polyester combination. If the tie looks synthetic don't buy it. This rule holds true for all apparel. Wool is another good tie material for cool weather. In hot weather a cotton material may be worn.

The design on the tie and the color should coordinate with the rest of your outfit. If you have trouble doing this, ask the haberdasher for help. Generally, the smaller the print, the more acceptable the tie. The tie that is most acceptable in America today is the muted paisley with a small print.

Most people in business consider the bow tie too eccentric. They are popular among scholars, some lawyers, and a few doctors. Bow ties have the advantage of not getting food or drink spilled on them as quickly as regular ties. If you rise high enough in rank, you can opt for the bow, otherwise no.

Never loosen your tie at the office; you may be mistaken for a liberal democrat.

WING-TIP WONDERS

The only safe shoe for men in corporate America is the black wing-tip, and for women, the medium or low-heeled pump. These shoes are acceptable in most organizations. Neither of these shoes are acceptable for evening wear. For men the tassel loafer is acceptable in a less conservative organization. The snap of the little tassel ends is as if your feet report for duty every time you take a step. The moccasin-style or penny loafer is too informal. It has been said, "Loafers are for loafers." For women, sling-backs or open-toed pumps are acceptable in a less conservative organization, but strappy sandals are inappropriate for office wear. Don't match your shoes exactly to your purse; they can match in color or texture, but not both. It's too contrived. For both men and women, your shoes should be darker than your suit.

Cordovan shoes are acceptable if you wear a burgundy tie or scarf with a matching belt. Choosing a belt color that matches your shoes is always the safest selection. Never wear cordovan shoes with a blue tie or scarf. Cordovan shoes go best with tan or beige, and some grays but few blues. Saddle shoes, e.g., half black and half cordovan or white, are worn by those who wish to be cheerleaders.

A woman bought shoes in the most fashionable store in the city. A few days later she returned there saying she couldn't walk in the shoes. The manager said, "Madam—people who have to walk don't buy shoes in this store."

SOCK IT TO ME

Socks should either be darker than or match the pants. Some gray pants are hard to match; black socks are acceptable with gray pants. Garters holding up socks are silly and passé. Wear "executive length" socks so that no hairy shank is exposed when you cross your legs. Socks should be a solid color. Stripes and argyles are not for business wear.

Women should wear neutral-colored pantyhose, with a color just a little darker than their skin tone. Fish nets, stockings with seams, and wildly colored stockings with designs on them are inappropriate for business. Never go bare-legged to the office. No matter how beautiful your legs or how hot the weather, this is an extremely unprofessional look.

One last precaution: in Arab nations you are expected to take off your shoes before entering the house. This is highly embarrassing if your feet stink or you have a hole in your hosiery. If you really want people to know where you stand, wear the same pair of socks for two weeks.

JEWELRY

When wearing jewelry use the KISS acronym... keep it simple, stupid. Multiple gold chains are fine on Mr. T. or for disco dancing, but not for work. For men, a small gold wedding band and a plain gold watch are acceptable. Women should follow the same KISS principle. Simple earrings, not the long kind that dangle, a simple gold or silver necklace (not diamonds or fashion jewelry) and a wedding ring are most acceptable. One of the worst faux paus an executive can make is to wear an ostentatious display of jewelry.

Avoid any symbols that give away your personal life: class

rings, Masonic rings, insignias on lapels, and most of all, leave
your peace symbol at home. Anything reminiscent of your
hippie days or school days lacks status and will brand you as
an immature rebel.

LAPELS AS WIDE AS DUMBO'S EARS

*A fashion ten years before its time is indecent. Ten
years after its time it is hideous. After a century it
becomes romantic.*

—JAMES LAVER

I was called by a vice president of a large organization with
the following request: "I want to promote Bud to the director's
position, but his clothes are so out of date, I would be embarrassed to introduce him to the guys upstairs. Would you
talk to him and take him shopping?" I talked to Bud about his
lime-green sports coat with the wide lapels. It was one of his
favorites. Bud told me that whenever he's down in the dumps,
he buys a new suit. I was wondering where he got them! With
some convincing, Bud consented to spending $2,000 on a new
wardrobe. The next day we went shopping. We carefully chose
him a wardrobe with color-coordinated ties and shirts. We then
went to the barber to have his long sideburns and walrus
mustache shaved off.

Bud looked and felt like a new man. He became more self-
confident and his career is blooming. He was introduced to
"the guys upstairs" and was instantly accepted.

Every few years the fashion industry changes our lapels and
ties. They widen them, narrow them, make them sharper,
etc. The wide lapels of the 1970s look out of date today. I
know a man who is so old that he has lived through three
revivals of the wide necktie. Hems rise and fall, some say,
according to the economy. Even though you have a perfectly

good suit, you must discard it or have it altered by a tailor. This is not to suggest that you should follow every fashion whim, but do make an effort to keep your wardrobe current. Jean Cocteau said, "Art produces ugly things which frequently become beautiful with time. Fashion, on the other hand, produces beautiful things which always become ugly with time."

Most people are reluctant to tell you that you look out of date, dorky, or dumb. Honest feedback is sometimes hard to come by particularly if you are in a position of authority. Two female executives who hadn't seen each other in a while met on the street one day. One said, "What have you done with your hair? It's terrible, it looks like a wig." The other said, "It is a wig." The first said, "Really? You could never tell."

SPECIAL CONSIDERATIONS FOR WOMEN

When dressing, women have more decisions to make than their male counterparts. A man stuffs his wallet in his pants pocket; no one knows if he is wearing black shoes with a brown wallet. Women must consider if their purse matches their shoes. Men don't have to decide on the earrings they are going to wear, how long their pants should be, or if their slip is showing. Men dress with comparative ease . . . "Should I wear my blue suit or my gray suit?" That's about the extent of a man's decision-making process in the morning.

In the 1970s Malloy's *Dress for Success* suggested clothing for women that has now become known as the "Uniform." The uniform's essential parts are: a dark two-button blazer, matching A-line skirt, white blouse, sheer tan stockings, and dark pumps. The entire suggested wardrobe was a variation of this theme, with the blazer being the centerpiece. Dressing was simpler then, with fewer decisions to make and less chance of dressing inappropriately. Today many women are giving their uniforms to the Salvation Army and turning to a more stylish professional look. Previously, the basic look was pre-determined and only the decisions that had to be made concerned accessories. Now decisions must be made on the basics as well as the accessories. You must decide if you want to wear a suit, coordinates, or a dress, and then decide on accessories. A complicated world is becoming even more complicated.

In today's busy world, many of us have to make hundreds of small and sometimes a few large decisions each day. The stress of making decisions builds up during the day. Before you have a chance to relax after making one decision, another issue must be resolved. The more decisions you have to make the more stress you have to endure. To eliminate these early morning decisions, why not have an outfit designated for each day of the week? The earrings, necklace, scarf, dress or skirt, blouse, stockings, shoes, and even your undergarments are all predetermined. Arrange these outfits in your closet in chronological order. On Monday mornings, put on your Monday outfit, on Tuesday, your Tuesday outfit and so on. When you need to bring your clothes to the cleaners, bring Monday and Tuesday's outfits on Wednesday so that they will be ready by Friday for you to pick them up and drop off your Wednesday, Thursday, and Friday outfits.

I know many of you will scoff at this idea . . . my wife did. Nevertheless, the fewer little decisions you have to make each day, the less stress build-up you will have to endure.

SPECIAL CONSIDERATIONS FOR REDNECKS

- Always buy your slacks to fit properly, so when you bend over people won't be able to see the tops of your underwear.
- Polyester anything is out, except for Bingo Night at the lodge.

- Don't wear bow ties if you are fat or if you have a square head.
- Socks should match, or at least be the same length.
- Carry an extra handkerchief to wipe the tobacco juice off your mouth.
- Make sure your name on the back of your belt is spelled correctly.
- If you run across a shirt with pictures of exotic birds on it, buy two. I'll take your extra.

CHAPTER FOUR:

SOCIAL SAVVY

HANDLING INTRODUCTIONS WITH FINESSE

WHEN TWO PEOPLE are introduced, they evaluate each other. The size of the person, how they are dressed, body language, eye contact, and many other visual clues are being processed. Our opinions about a person are formed within the first few seconds of meeting him. Remember when hitchhiking was popular? While hurtling down the freeway at seventy miles per hour, we could see a hitchhiker, evaluate him, and decide if we wanted to pick him up. This whole evaluative process took about three seconds. About ninety percent of what you will ever feel about a person is decided within those precious few seconds and once opinions are formed it is very hard to change them. The following are a few tips on introducing others and being introduced:

- When introducing others, use both their first and last names.

- Use "Mr." when introducing a man in formal situations or in deference to age or position.
- Use "Ms." when marital status is unknown or irrelevant. In most business situations "Ms." is appropriate.
- "Miss" is used if the woman is unmarried and "Mrs." if she is married. These prefixes are appropriate in some social situations and in deference to age.
- Most people who have earned their terminal degree like to be introduced as "Dr."

Add a bit of nonpersonal information about the person immediately following their name. For example, "I would like for you to meet Mr. Elmer Fudd. He is an extraordinary duck hunter."

GIVE ME FIVE

After the verbal exchange comes the physical contact . . . the handshake. Americans shake hands less frequently than people from any other country. This is unfortunate because physical touching when people meet is important. The touch adds either confirming or discordant data after our visual senses have made an evaluation.

Since ancient times, handshakes were used as gestures of peace. An open hand indicated it held no weapon. During the Roman Empire the clasp was made of the forearm, as a means of making certain that no weapon was hidden in the sleeve. As time passed, the handshake evolved to the hand.

When shaking hands, look the person in the eye, hold out your hand, and give a firm handshake. Two pumps are usually enough. If you are shaking hands with a big burly type, make sure you push your hand deep into the brute's hand so that the webs of your thumbs touch. Otherwise you may find yourself grimacing as your knuckles are squeezed in a vise-like grip.

The wimpy handshake is the worst, unless you are in England. The English have a much less firm handshake and the distance between the two shakers is increased. In America, no one likes a limp handshake.

For some people the wet handshake is the worst. As an interviewer, I considered a wet hand indicated that the interviewee was nervous and may really want the job. In most situations it's best not to have a wet, clammy hand. If you know you have this problem, wipe you hand discretely on your pants or skirt before the handshake.

A cold wet hand is even worse than just a wet hand. When at a function where drinks are served, carry your drink in your left hand. Leave the right hand dry, warm, and available for shaking.

Those of us who work in sedentary occupations must be careful not to let our hands get too weak to give a nice firm handshake. The only other alternative is to move to England.

Today, business etiquette is still struggling to define how a man and woman should shake hands. Generally, men are a little uncomfortable with this situation. Back in the era of buggies and bustles, it was considered improper for a man to offer a woman his hand. He was expected to wait for her to make the offer, then he was expected to give her a delicate half-shake. Some women today consider this old-time civility an insult. Today it is acceptable for either party to extend the hand first. Nevertheless, the tension prevails. To relieve the tension of the situation a woman should offer her hand first. This defuses the situation. Simply offer your hand and give a firm hand shake. Don't forget to make eye contact.

"Hip" hand shakes are perfectly acceptable . . . if you are dealing in drugs.

KISSING

Many people in social situations kiss when meeting. Usually the kiss is just a peck on the cheek or it may be an air kiss. An air kiss is when two people offer first one cheek, and then the other, kissing the air next to each side of the face. The regular kiss is still shaded with romanticism in our society and is not a fully accepted business behavior. In New York and a few other eastern cities the air kiss is gaining ground when used in certain business/social situations. Don't try this in Texas.

The air kiss can be difficult to execute with someone who doesn't know what you're doing. The recipient may not have the foreknowledge that you are going to follow through with an air kiss on the other side. The result may create a clumsy moment of embarrassment. Handshakes are the safest, most universally accepted form of business greetings.

The boss said, "Who said you could neglect your office duties just because I give you a little kiss now and then?" His secretary said, "My attorney."

PERSONAL SPACE

Personal space is the area immediately around the body, and the invasion of one's personal space is disturbing. When people stand less than two and a half feet from us during a conversation, we feel uncomfortable. The amount of space we need varies from culture to culture. Americans and the British tend to require more space than other cultures. Country folks require more space than people from large cities, but your country cousin isn't as threatened by people invading it. Country folk like to touch people when conversing, city people don't like to be touched. Touching for most big-city people starts three to six inches from the body.

In some Arab cultures, there's a saying that if you trust a man you should give him your breath. It's unfortunate that those cultures have yet to adopt Listerine. Distrust and offense will permeate your relationship if you back off from the invading Arab.

Be aware of how much space you give to others. We usually don't think about how close we stand or how much we touch another person. The person whose space you're invading will probably not realize why they are uncomfortable, they will just have a vague feeling of intrusion. For example: when your boss walks up behind you, leans over you, and then sits on your desk he is nonverbally saying, "I'm in charge here, and I have the right to invade your space."

Schizophrenics and violent prisoners have been found to have larger body–buffer zones. One researcher found that violent prisoners had zones of 22.3 square feet, compared with 7.0 for nonviolent prisoners. Their zones were larger from behind than in front. There was evidence that they feared physical or homosexual attack. The point is, if you feel your boss is dishonest, violent, or nuts, give him lots of space, and never approach him from the rear.

PERSONAL TERRITORY

This is an area that an individual owns, has exclusive use of, or controls. This space provides privacy, or social intimacy. House, car, and office are examples of areas one may include in one's personal territory. A territory may be established simply by repeated occupation of a particular seat or table. In most homes each member of the family has a bed (or a designated side of a bed), chair, and place at the dinner table. Remember when Archie Bunker would come home from work and say, "Get outta my chair Meathead?"

Personal territory in your own office can be used against you in a negotiation session. If the negotiator walks into your office and takes your chair, you will be thrown a little off balance. If you can keep your cool about this you can turn the tables and use your office for its home field advantage. Having people come to your office or desk for meetings or negotiation gives you the upper hand. You are more powerful in your own territory than the person who has come to you. Even if all you have is a cubicle, it is still best to meet on your own turf.

First of all, it is your playhouse. You exercise control over a meeting in your office that you don't have elsewhere.

Second, because this is your personal territory, a meeting on your turf brings with it a sense of "invasion" by the other party. There is tension there, however subliminal it may be. By being polite and making the other person feel comfortable, you can diffuse the tension and develop a certain amount of trust and confidence before the meeting begins.

If you want to try an experiment to test this personal territory theory try this: the next time you eat with a friend, wait until your friend isn't looking, and discretely set your water glass down on his or her side of the table. See how long it takes them to notice it and place it on your side of the table.

When in a restaurant it's best to use the Billy the Kid motto: "Always sit with your back to the wall." He sat that way because he didn't want someone shooting him in the back. He had more control over his personal territory. In the same way, you have more control over those seated at your table with their backs exposed. More of the table becomes your territory.

REMEMBERING NAMES

Many times we do not remember someone's name because we don't really hear it during the introduction. If you do not clearly hear the person's name, ask them to repeat it. Once you've heard the name clearly, a good mnemonic to use to remember the name is to make a fantastical association. For example: Al Duckworth may be remembered by visualizing a lone duck with $100 in its bill; Vern Crawford can be visualized by a crawfish fording a stream with a piece of fern in its claw; and Harriett Handshaw as a woman eating her own hair while holding a shawl in her hand. Some visualizations are best done by associating the name with an outstanding physical characteristic, for example: Linda as lovely Linda, or John as big bad John.

Some people say, "I never forget a face but I have trouble remembering names," while others have no trouble remembering names. People who easily remember names are not necessarily smarter. Some people are right-brain dominant; they think in pictures. Left-brain dominant people think in words.

Right-brain dominant people benefit most from the visualization mnemonic, while left-brained people usually can't visualize very well. They do best by simply saying the name subvocally seven times.

When someone forgets your name as he is introducing you, save the forgetful soul some painful embarrassment by quickly supplying your name. Should you forget someone's name as you introduce him, pause and roll your eyes up. He should get the hint and supply his name. If he doesn't get the hint, ask him for it.

WHEN TO STAND

Always stand to greet a client, a senior executive, or when being introduced. It is polite to stand to greet anyone who comes into your office, with the exception of a secretary or a coworker who comes in regularly. When you are waiting at a restaurant for your dinner guests, it's also polite to stand when they arrive.

Two men were seated on a crowded bus; one noticed that the other had his eyes closed. "What's the matter, pal?" he asks. "You sick?" "No, I'm all right. It's just that I hate to see women standing."

BE A SPORT ABOUT SPORTS

When invited to attend the football draft, don't think this is an invitation to go have a few draft beers. Many men establish a common ground by talking about sports. To avoid looking like a complete nincompoop, you need to learn a few basics about sports. Things like: in what seasons the various sports are played, the names of your local professional ball teams, and that Monday nights are sacred for football fans.

You may want to learn to speak the language of the sports favored by your organization, and then again you may not. In favor of knowing something about sports, you may save yourself some embarrassment and be able to join in on an occasional semiboring conversation.

If you dislike sports and refuse to learn anything about them, the least you can do is memorize the following quotes:

"Pro football is like nuclear warfare. There are no winners, only survivors."
—FRANK GIFFORD

"I hate sports as rabidly as a person who likes sports hates common sense."
—H. L. MENCKEN

"Golf is a good walk spoiled."
—YOGI BERRA

"A sportsman is a man who, every now and then, simply has to get out and kill something. Not that he's cruel. He wouldn't hurt a fly. It's not big enough."

—ANONYMOUS

When playing company-sponsored sports or when playing a sport like tennis or golf with a company employee, good sportsmanship is essential. Many business relationships are forged in the locker room and on the playing fields. Your teammates and opponents will judge what kind of business behavior they can expect from you by your behavior in a competitive sport.

If you are not good in a sport, don't play it until you have attained at least minimal competency. You could look like a bungling idiot in front of your business associates. Your image in the sport may carry over to your professional image. If you intend to play golf or tennis, don't show up in a thrown-together outfit. Dress with the same care you would when going to the office. Some companies take their sports very seriously and will not appreciate you losing the game for them. Better to select a sport you like and may have some skill in, and take some lessons from a professional.

It is imperative that you have good manners when playing sports. A courteous sportsman is a good winner, always praising the efforts of his opponent and never saying anything that is belittling. He never says, "I'm sure you would have beaten me, Roseanne, if you weren't so fat," or "You noticed that I still beat you, Chris, even though you lied about that ball being out of bounds." A good winner never tries to fleece his opponent as in, "Come on Roseanne, lets play double or nothing . . . I'll give you a chance to catch up."

It's also important to know how to be a good loser. A good loser shakes the hand of his opponent and thanks her for a good game. He should never swear loudly, throw sports equipment on the ground or blame the officials.

Remember, when playing company-sponsored sports your image and perhaps your job is at stake.

Nick was invited to a company-sponsored softball game that was attended by several higher ranking executives. When the game started Nick confidently assumed the pitcher's mound. (The executives thought, "confidence—that's a good trait.") Nick wound up and threw his fastball. Tim at the bat was absolutely intimidated by Nick's fastball. Nick jeered at him and said, "What's the matter Timmy, scared of a little softball?" (The executives thought, "meanness—that's not so good.") Tim gritted his teeth and hit a center-field line drive. Nick was so fast he managed to catch the ball, throw to first base and Tim was called out. ("Speed—that's good.") The next batter up was Big John, a tall, well-muscled, ex-professional minor league player. When Big John got up to bat, Nick called time out. Nick went to the dugout, took out a jar of Vaseline and rubbed it on the ball. Nick thought he wasn't seen. (An executive saw him and motioned for the other executives to observe Nick. "Cheating—that's not so good.") Nick's team won the game but he lost his credibility and was fired a few months later for having his hand in the company till.

Assertiveness, speed, teamwork, and determination are assets in business and in sports. Meanness and cheating are not. Sports do not necessarily build character, they reveal it.

AIR TRAVEL TIPS

When on a business trip, do not check pieces of baggage that you will need on the first day of your arrival. Pack a small bag that you can carry on the plane. You may include your appointment book, a fresh shirt or blouse, toiletries, and a briefcase with important papers. If the airline looses your luggage, they can usually recover it within twenty-four hours. With the bag that you carried on, you can survive that long.

A friend told me that the last time he flew, the airline lost his luggage. He said that he was used to that, but this time he was a little suspicious—the guy at the baggage claim was wearing his clothes.

In your appointment book list your credit card numbers (without identifying the company), the numbers to call to report lost or stolen cards, frequent-flier numbers, and your passport number (with date and place of issue). Also list confirmation numbers for hotels and rental cars as well as telephone numbers of where you will be staying and the place where you will be doing business. Tear off the receipt from your airline ticket with serial numbers, flight numbers and dates, and store it in the pocket of your appointment book. If you lose your ticket or just want to confirm reservations, having this information will help.

You never know whom you will meet when waiting for a flight or who will be in the seat next to you. This may be a good time for networking, but then again your acquaintance may not want to talk. If the person next to you seems absorbed in work or reading, it's best to cut the chatter. If you are seated next to a loquacious person and you would rather have peace and quiet you might say, "This report must be ready by the time we deplane, I really must work on it." When the meal is served and you can't work or read, let the talkative person release his or her wagging tongue.

If you're sitting next to someone who has a fear of flying, lend him a helping hand. Just talk to him in a calm, reassuring way. Explain any sudden noises, such as the landing gear being lowered or flying into a bit of turbulence. You may remind him of a comment made by Satchel Paige, "Airplanes may kill you, but they ain't likely to hurt you."

With flights always delayed or canceled, you wonder why they bother to put out a schedule. Of course, they need something to base their delays on. It's helpful if you have an O.A.G.—a pocket guide to all flights—in case you have to reschedule. That way, you will not have to spend hours on the phone, waiting for a reservation clerk.

If your flight has been delayed en route and you are late for an important meeting, it can be helpful to very quietly explain your need to deplane immediately to an attendant. It may be possible for the attendant to make sure you are one of the first off the plane.

Dress in comfortable clothes but don't dress like a bum. Leave your beat-up old T-shirt and sawed-off jeans at home. Slacks and a long-sleeved blouse or shirt are more appropriate. On long flights many people suffer from swollen feet. Wear comfortable shoes that will allow for some swelling.

The best way to avoid jet lag on long flights is to avoid alcohol and drink a lot of water. What many travelers think of as jet lag is in reality a hangover. It takes less alcohol to get loaded at 37,000 feet than it does at sea level.

The food served in the coach class section can sometimes be on the spare side. If you are on a long flight and are really hungry, the meal may be less than filling. In this case simply ask the flight attendant if there are any meals left over. On most flights at least one person will be too nervous to eat. The flight attendant will gladly give you the extra meal at no charge. Requests for a special diet for health or religious reasons can be accommodated by the airlines if you mention your needs when buying your ticket.

When deplaning it is polite to tell your flight attendants, "Thank you." They have a difficult job: a flight attendant on a New Orleans–Los Angeles flight had her hands full fending off two persistent drunks. The one seated in the front of the plane was doing his best to persuade her to come to his apartment. At the rear, the second drunk was trying to get an invitation to her apartment. As the plane headed for the runway, the front-seat pest handed her a key and a slip of paper on which he had written his address. "Here's the key and my address," he whispered. "See you tonight?" "Okay," she said, smiling sweetly as she headed for the drunk at the rear. She handed him the key and slip of paper and said, "Don't be late."

THE MORNING AFTER

Never schedule an important meeting the day after you have consumed large quantities of beer, rum punch, and margueritas.

I take Mardi Gras seriously, and so do many of my friends. My wife and I get up at 6:00 A.M., put on our costumes, by 6:30 about a dozen of our friends come over and we hit the streets by 7:00. We walk over to Commander's Palace to follow Pete Fountain's Half Fast Marching Band. We party and drink all day and we don't stop until the last parade (Comus) has past. Then we go back to our house and the party continues.

In New Orleans Mardi Gras day is a legal holiday: unfortunately the day after isn't a holiday. Twelve years ago we had our usual Mardi Gras celebration and the day after I was not at my best, to say the least, but I made it to work anyway. My boss and a humorless executive from accounting decided the three of us should have a meeting. Both of these fellows were recent transplants from Ohio and had not yet learned that serious business is not conducted in New Orleans the day after Mardi Gras.

I went to the meeting, still slightly cross-eyed and barely able to keep my breakfast down. The meeting went on forever, the voices melted together, and I could barely keep my head off the conference table. After what seemed like hours of torture the meeting was adjourned at noon and I staggered off to my office for a nice snooze.

The next day I had no recollection of what we had talked about, or what kind of work these two higher-ups had dumped on me. I was sure they had agreed for me to do something, but I had no idea what I was supposed to do.

My strategy was to play it cool. I walked into my boss's office and asked, "Well, what did you think about the meeting yesterday?" He said, "What do you mean what do I think, what do you think about it?"

There I was, bitten by a big bad mosquito again. I did learn the lesson. I always schedule a vacation day the day after Mardi Gras. If you know you are going to party hearty on a holiday, schedule the day after for recovery. Why go to work if you don't have a brain to bring with you?

CHAPTER FIVE

PHYSICAL APPEARANCE

THERE IS A stereotype that has a great advantage in the business world. People who are good-looking, male, white, with an athletic build, and come from an upper-middle-class family, have a birthright advantage over all others. When combined with some acting ability and average intelligence they can become juggernauts in the corporate world. Former President Ronald Reagan is the archetype of this image. If you weren't born with all of these attributes, perhaps this chapter will help.

THE THREE-LETTER "F" WORD

Most Americans feel fat, and most of them really are. Since you're reading this book right now instead of jogging, you're probably fat. Since fat has become so widespread, I decided to do a special mosquito just for them and ignore the skinny, tall, and short people.

We consume tons of "lite" foods, go to health spas to lose weight, and wear vertical stripes to hide what we can't lose. According to research done by National Personnel Associates, overweight applicants—both men and women—have more difficulty finding jobs than do their thinner peers. Fat people are discriminated against. They are called slovenly, lazy, and are expected to be jovial at all times.

Most men, when they meet another man for the first time, or when they see an acquaintance after a relatively lengthy interval, look or at least glance at the other man's stomach. They compare it with their own.

It has been said, "You can never be too rich or too thin." Everyone knows, to lose weight you must diet and exercise. As Mark Twain so aptly said: "The only way to keep your health is to eat what you don't want, drink what you don't like, and do what you'd rather not."

A patient came into the doctor's office for an examination and after it was over, the fellow said: "All right, Doc. Now I don't want you to give me a bunch of tongue-twisting scientific talk. Just tell me straight out in plain English what my problem is."

"All right," said the physician, "you're fat and you're lazy."

"Fine," said the patient, "now give me the scientific terms so I can tell my friends."

If you have surrendered the battle of the bulge there are still some things you can do to make yourself look less fat.

For Men
- Stay away from patch pockets; they attract the eye to the hips.
- If you wear a vest, make sure it does not pull or gap.
- Stay with the center-vent jackets, rather than double-vent.
- Do not wear trousers with cuffs.

- Make sure your shirt collar fits properly.
- Stay with dark colors and thin pinstripes for suits.
- Never wear tight clothes.
- Wear suits instead of blazers with contrasting pants.
- Wear a two-button jacket rather than the European three-button style.
- Do not wear double-breasted jackets.

By taking these suggestions you can move from looking like Archie Bunker or John Goodman to looking like Raymond Burr or Orson Wells.

For Women
- Wear narrow rather than wide belts.
- Avoid the unbelted sack look.
- Avoid lots of ruffles and flounces.
- Don't wear clothes with big details such as large bows or sleeves.
- Keep jewelry and accessories simple.
- Wear woven fabrics rather than clingy knits.
- Select fabrics that are soft and thin, avoid heavy or bulky fabrics.
- Fit, not what size you wear, is the most critical element.
- Keep one basic color tone to your outfit.
- The styles that will be most flattering are: skirted suits, classic jackets and A-line skirts.
- Choose solid colors for jackets and small prints for dresses.

As Frank O'Hare says, "It is easy to be beautiful; it is difficult to appear so."

POOR POSTURE

Good posture can somewhat compensate for being fat. People will say, "She's fat but she carries it well." I am six feet-four-inches tall and was hounded by my mother to hold my shoulders back. Slumping is a common malady among self-conscious teens who tower above their peers. All the harassment did little good.

Upper-middle-class people hold their shoulders back and their heads erect. Their lower-middle-class counterparts have slumped shoulders and hold their heads down, forcing them to have a rolling motion when they walk (commonly referred to as the "pimp stroll"). As implied at the beginning of this chapter, the UMC are seen as more competent, intelligent, and beautiful than are the LMC, but don't be discouraged if you were not born with these UMC qualities: with practice, you can fake it.

The cure for slumping is the Opera Singer's Stance. When standing making a presentation, in a grocery line, or wherever else, assume the OSS: place your right foot slightly in front of the left foot with the ball of your left foot near the arch of your right foot. With this footing your body will be forced to stand straight. The entire rib cage opens up and you can breathe more deeply and project your voice more forcefully. If this doesn't work, try the U.S. Army.

If you slump when you stand, you probably also slump when you are seated. You may feel that slumping is just a relaxing way to sit; to the person with whom you are conversing it means that he is not important enough for you to pay full attention to what he is saying. Even if he has your rapt attention, your body language is telling the other person that you are not actively involved in the conversation. To appear as if you are paying attention, look the speaker in the eye and arch your head and shoulders and lean forward. Jay Leno assumes this posture when he interviews a guest on the "Tonight" show.

How assertive we appear is determined to a large degree by our posture or body language. Dr. Albert Mehrabian, in his book *Silent Messages* (Belmont, CA: Wadsworth, 1981), divides communication skills into three components: verbals, vocals and nonverbals. Verbals are the words we use to communicate a message and would seem to be the most important. Dr. Mehrabian's experiments indicated that only 7 percent of what we say is communicated by verbals. Vocals, the tone of voice used to convey a message, communicate 38 percent of what we say. Nonverbals, the physical movements, posture, gestures, and facial expressions, communicate 55 percent of what we say.

To project an air of confidence, you must move with confidence. The confident person indicates this by a strong stride, good posture, and a sense of energy or enthusiasm. To create an air of confidence when making an entrance, move with your rib cage upward. Do not slump over or pitch forward. Hold your head up, keep your shoulders square, your back straight, and smile. Hold your briefcase in your left hand leaving the right hand free to shake hands.

When walking to the boardroom or to the restroom, you should look as if you're walking fast. If you walk with a shuffle and a slump, you are going to look tired, depressed, lazy, or bored. If you aren't carrying anything, let your arms swing freely at you side. If you are carrying papers, hold them at your side rather than clutching them to your chest. Female executives should hold their derrière and stomach in place, rather than swinging them from side to side. You want your walk to convey power, confidence and determination. Research has shown that people who walk with confidence and determination are less likely to get mugged when walking in dangerous areas. This same walk will help you navigate through dangerous corporate corridors. Your style of walking can get you where you want to go . . . in more ways than one.

To change one's posture requires constant vigilance and effort. If you are going to convince anyone, your posture must be consistent, not something you turn on and off when the occasion arises.

A young woman applied for a job as a cigarette girl at a fancy nightclub. The owner decided to audition her. He let her have the job for one night to see how she would do. At the beginning of the evening she walked around with perfect posture, shoulders back and her head held high, saying "Cigarettes and almonds." About four hours later, her shoulders had slumped over a little, her head wasn't in the air, and she was going from table to table saying, "Cigarettes and ammans." Finally, at the end of the night, she was sitting down, slumped over, yelling "Nuts and butts."

SPIT & POLISH

Keep your shoes shined, your teeth cleaned, and wash often. One technique that a chief economist used in a large organization was to keep an extra pair of highly shined shoes in his filing cabinet. When the big boss called, he changed shoes. This is probably beyond the call of duty but well-shined shoes have been a military hallmark of excellence since World War I.

YOU MAKE ME WANNA PUKE

There are many human functions that people find objectionable. Some of these are: spitting, picking your nose, belching, farting, toothpicking with fingers (some also find toothpicking with a toothpick offensive), reaming out your ears with your fingers, scratching crotch or buttocks, knuckle popping, scalp or beard scratching, fingernail biting or clipping, chewing on your pen or ear piece of your glasses, twisting your hair, gum popping, and talking with your mouth full. The list goes on *ad infinitum*. All of these things are somehow related to hygiene and should be avoided in public.

It is never appropriate to do grooming or hygiene chores in the view of your coworkers. The desk is not the place to fix your makeup or do your nails, for it only reminds people that you need grooming. Men are the worst offenders with nail clippers; the noise sets many people's teeth on edge.

When you are with someone that has obnoxious personal habits, it is appropriate to discreetly tell them about it. Many of these behaviors are habits that the offender is not even aware of doing.

BROWN TEETH

Teeth stained by coffee, tea, cigarette smoke, or infrequent brushing are disfiguring. Besides, all that plaque can rot your teeth. The people you meet notice your teeth within the first sixty seconds of your encounter. Many business people keep a toothbrush, toothpaste, and a container of dental floss in their desk drawer. Brushing your teeth after lunch in the company restroom is perfectly acceptable and also very smart. Get your teeth cleaned every six months, or more often if you are a smoker.

COLOGNES

Colognes that are overly powerful should be avoided. Strong scents can be annoying to people if their senses are assailed frequently during the day. People who wear strong after shave lotions and perfumes do not consider these odors offensive, since the primary reason for using them is to please the senses. If you are in frequent contact with someone who does wear a fragrance that is stronger than you can tolerate, it is reasonable to ask him or her to tone it down. Since the fragrance is not a bodily produced scent, it is not necessary to worry about offending someone by asking him or her to relieve you of the irritation. It is not rude to wear a cologne to the office when it is applied in moderation. Personal scents and fragrances should be light, pleasant and nondistinctive. Above all, stay away from patchoulie.

YOU STINK

The author was asked by a female executive to tell a male coworker that he had body odor. She did not want to confront him because he was hot-tempered and took offense easily, particularly when criticized by a woman. This was a highly embarrassing situation for all involved.

I took a deep breath and asked the odoriferous man to come into my office. With him seated on the other side of my desk, I told him point blank that there had been complaints about his body odor. The man was totally surprised. He said, "But I shower every day, how can that be?" I asked him how often he washed his shirts. He said, "I have five shirts that I rotate for about a month, and then I have them washed." I encouraged him to wash his shirts weekly and with his compliance, the problem was solved.

Sometimes it is hard to recognize your own body odor and friends are reluctant to say anything. Even if you don't perspire heavily, you need a deodorant that you apply daily. Since your body chemistry changes periodically, you may need to switch brands accordingly. In tense situations we produce more odorous perspiration than in exercise. If you know you are going to have a tense day, you may want to make an extra application of deodorant. Remember: if cleanliness is next to godliness, who do you think uncleanliness is next to?

TOILET TRAINING

I lived in California's Marin County for a few years, during which we had a severe drought. Good citizens were encouraged to not fill their swimming pools, to take "Navy Showers," to put a brick in their toilet and not to flush it unless absolutely necessary. Being a good citizen I practiced water conservation and the practice became a habit. When I moved to Louisiana, water conservation was not an issue, but my conservation habits remained.

One morning I was using a urinal next to a coworker of slightly higher rank. After I voided, I did not flush: the other fellow did flush, and I thought, "How wasteful." The other fellow was not impressed with my urinary habits and actually told my boss about the incident. Again yours truly was bitten by a mosquito. The moral . . . always flush.

After flushing always wash your hands.

Two fellows were using urinals side by side. When one fellow finished he promptly washed his hands. The other fellow did not. The first fellow said, "At Harvard they taught us to wash before exiting the restroom." The second fellow said, "At Yale they taught us not to urinate on our hands."

HAIR LENGTH FOR WOMEN

Just as men should not wear long hair in corporate America neither should women. Hair that falls below the shoulders is considered hippie-ish or schoolgirlish, time consuming, and out of date. I personally like long hair. When I met my wife, she had hair down to her waist. Today she works in corporate America and accordingly, wears her hair to her shoulders. Some religions teach that because a woman's hair is her "crowning glory" it should never be cut. Of course you can have long hair if you pull it back in a bun . . . like my grand-mother.

BALDNESS ISN'T BAD

There's no time for a man to recover his hair that grows bald by nature.
— WILLIAM SHAKESPEARE

During my entire life I have been exceedingly healthy; not through heredity, but through effort. I eat oatmeal every morning, salads at lunch, and low cholesterol dinners. I run every day and gave up cigarettes fifteen years ago. I am the right weight for my height and I have my teeth cleaned every six months. I have a full head of hair and my barber told me I would never have to worry about going bald.

On July 12, 1988 at 11:00 P.M, I had a grand-mal seizure. I awoke in a hospital bed and was told I had a malignant brain tumor that had to be removed. It was quite a shock, because, as I previously said, I was the picture of health until this tumor made itself known. To make a long story short, I had the surgery, radiation treatments, and all my hair fell out. That is where I got first-hand experience at being bald.

Being bald was not all that bad, especially during the summer. Women seemed to like it and would want to rub my head. Men told me it made me look more dynamic, like Yul Brynner and Telly Savalas. I even started going around with a sucker in my mouth. Eventually the hair grew back, my health returned, and I resumed my healthy lifestyle.

The point of telling you this bit of personal history is to lend credence to my theory that bald is beautiful. Some men try to hide their baldness and end up looking like an insecure nerd. Men spend thousands on hair transplants and toupées when what they need to realize is that many women like bald men. By age thirty-five, 60 percent of the male population is losing its hair—that's fifty million Americans. Perhaps you can take some comfort in knowing—you are not alone.

Men have always lamented their thinning hair. Aristotle was bald and hated it. So was Hippocrates. Hippocrates, the father of medicine, applied female sheep's urine to his bald spot. The Romans plastered their heads with chicken dung. This fertilizer treatment made plants grow, but didn't work on hair. At the turn of the century, a hot mail-order item was the Evans VacuumCap, which essentially sucked your scalp like a vacuum cleaner. Allegedly, it stimulated the blood supply to the scalp to promote new hair growth. This didn't work either.

The 1970s brought us hair implants. They should have been called artificial hair implants to distinguish them from real hair transplants. In this procedure a twelve-inch strand of artificial hair was threaded through the scalp and knotted. This process was repeated until the bald spot was covered. Eventually, the scalp would reject the artificial hair and if it wasn't removed immediately infection would follow. The Food and Drug Administration outlawed this practice after two men died from the procedure.

I recently met a man at a party who told me that he used to hang upside down in a doorway by gravity boots with hooks. He said he did this for twenty minutes every day for two years. He held the belief that if he hung up side down the circulation to his scalp would improve. As a result he said his hair stopped falling out, but he didn't grow any new hair. He started having frequent headaches and his doctor told him that hanging upside down increases the likelihood of a stroke.

Most baldness is caused by two factors: the baldness gene can be passed down from your mother or your father; or, the cause is testosterone. Testosterone is that hormone that

makes you a macho man. That's why few women go bald—
they don't have much testosterone. Have you ever seen a
bald eunuch?

Today men have several options, some of them are expensive, some can create major medical problems and some make
you look like a cheap toupée.

Cheap toupées always look like cheap toupées. If you buy
a cheap toupée you'll end up loosing hair that isn't even yours.
Everyone will know you are wearing it and once aware, they
will focus their attention on the toupée rather than on you.
Even with extremely expensive toupées, the façade cannot be
maintained in a daily working relationship. Expensive toupées
end up looking like expensive toupées.

So the top of your head is bald, but you have plenty of
hair around you ears. Why not let the hair around your ears
grow extremely long and then just comb it over the bald
spot; of course your part must be a little lower, but what
the heck. This tactic never works; it's more obvious than a
toupée. Have you ever seen the wind blow the hair all the
way over the bald head so that if flaps down on the other
side? I had a boss that wore this style; it was embarrassing
to both of us.

Some men resort to hairweaving. This is comparable to
blending a toupée in with your hair semipermanently. A nylon
lattice is placed over the bald spot, and surrounding hairs
are braided and woven around the edges of the lattice to
hold it firmly in place. Strands of your own hair, supplemented
by synthetic and/or human hair, are woven into the lattice
base until it is concealed by hair. The problem with a hairweave is that it becomes loose as your natural hair grows.
A hairweave can cost as much as $1,200; an adjustment costs
about $50 and takes several hours and is only good for about
six weeks.

Hair transplants are time-consuming, painful, and expensive.
Only the truly desperate resort to this treatment. It is only

effective for small bald patches that are not the result of an ongoing pattern of baldness. Small sections of hair, skin, follicles, and fat, called "plugs" are taken from the back and sides of the head and surgically implanted into the bald areas. Afterwards, the plugs start pumping out hair. Transplants are not used to produce a full head of hair, only to fill small bald spots. Your natural hair continues to recede around the plug. The average head has 100,000 individual hairs, the average plug has fifteen hairs; in one session you may optimistically hope for 500 plugs. That's 7500 hairs, or 7.5 percent of a full head of hair. Each session costs between $500 and $1,000 and there's always lots of blood. After a session you have to wear a gauze bandage around your head, and everyone you meet asks, "Gee, what happened to you, did you have brain surgery?"

Rogaine—better living through chemistry? Originally developed as a treatment for high blood pressure, Rogaine has been hailed as the solution to baldness. When applied topically, it stimulates dormant hair follicles beneath the skin to grow hair. Rogaine is the only FDA approved medication for growing hair. You can't buy it off the shelf yet, but you can get it through a dermatologist. It must be applied twice a day for as long as you want hair.

Rogaine only works on the crown or back of your head. If you have a growing forehead, Rogaine is not for you. It works best on men who have been balding less than ten years and whose bald spot is no bigger than four inches. After every use your hands should be thoroughly washed, otherwise hair will grow on your palms. The cost will be about $60 a month for the rest or your life.

Look at baldness this way: having hair is not going to change your life. Besides, many women like bald-headed men; baldness can enhance your appearance by making you seem more dynamic; and as a real bonus you are helping out the Lord. The Bible says, "The very hairs on your head are all numbered," but each year it gets a little easier for the Lord to take inventory.

GRAY HAIR & WRINKLES

The double standard comes galloping in without restraint. The inequities keep increasing as a woman ages. The graying temples of a man enhance his image, adding a touch of sophistication. For some reason, the same gray in a woman's hair rarely has the same positive effect.

I personally like a touch of gray in a woman's hair. I feel more comfortable with her and feel that she has more of life's experiences to share. Unfortunately, research has shown that the gray in a woman's hair usually serves only to indicate advancing years and conjures up maternal images.

The deep lines in a man's face denote experience, character and strength. They don't do that for a woman. Research has shown that the older woman faces greater job discrimination than the older man.

Fortunately there are things a woman can do. Things such as: avoiding the sun, quitting smoking, exercise, hair dyes, choosing the right clothes, Retin-A cream and moisturizers, and for the adventurous . . . plastic surgery. Doing what you can to preserve a youthful appearance is not vain or superficial. It makes good business sense. If you are going to work in a corporation, your image is always going to be vitally important. You can't sit back at forty-five and feel that you can rest on your laurels. If you stop caring about your image, you will communicate that you have given up, that you are too old and tired to care. When you give up on your image you will not only appear old and tired, you will feel that way too.

Phyllis Diller on her sixty-second birthday: "I'm really

only thirty-five because I have been taking birthday control pills."

ANYONE CAN QUIT SMOKING, IT TAKES CHUTZPAH TO STAND UP TO CANCER

Smoking is a shocking thing—blowing smoke out of our mouths into other people's mouths, eyes, and noses, and having the same thing done to us.
                                          —SAMUEL JOHNSON

SURGEON GENERAL'S WARNING: Quitting Smoking Now Greatly Reduces Serious Risks to Your Health.

Nonsmokers are more likely to be hired than smokers when both are equally qualified for a job. Robert Half International Inc., a recruiting firm, queried 100 personnel directors. Though 70 percent had no preference, 25 percent would hire the nonsmoker if equally qualified. Nonsmokers and especially ex-smokers can be quite militant about smokers polluting their air. In most other nations, most adults smoke. Nonsmoking rules do not exist. The exception is in Islamic countries, which are nonsmoking. Don't press your nonsmoking ethic on your hosts. In America nonsmoking militarism is rampant.

I successfully used Aversion Therapy to quit smoking cigarettes. A fifteen-year, pack-a-day habit is not easy to quit, but this technique was highly effective. The first step is to pick a date when you resolve to quit smoking. One week prior to that date, double your smoking rate, with a brand you can't stand. If you have a pack-a-day habit, force yourself to smoke two packs a day. Continue this forced smoking for a week. Save your cigarette butts and put them in clear glass containers. After one week, my teeth were yellow, my lungs were congested, and I gladly quit smoking. When tempted by a relapse, simply open your clear glass jar containing your old butts, and inhale deeply. The smell is so revolting, the temptation quickly disappears. The only draw-back to this technique is that if it doesn't work, you may be stuck with a habit twice as strong as your old habit.

Another smoking cessation method suggested by an Army doctor is as follows: Each day the smoker postpones for one hour longer that first cigarette. On the first day, as many cigarettes as desired may be smoked. On the second day, the first cigarette is put off for one hour, but after that the smoker consumes as many as he wishes. On the third day, no cigarettes are smoked until two hours after rising, but, again, as many thereafter as are craved. Smoking will cease in about two weeks.

The theory is that if a smoker can consume an unlimited number of cigarettes after the period of abstinence, he or she loses fear of the program.

If you must smoke, hide the fact. Smokers and overweight people are the two most discriminated against groups in America. Smoking is hard to hide; you must have your teeth frequently cleaned, brush and use a strong mouth wash after every smoke. If you must smoke while at work, confine your smoking to your own office and have a smoke-eater device to dispel lingering odors. When someone else is in your office and you have the urgent need to light up, always ask if the other person minds. Nonsmokers should not be offensive in expressing their resentment toward smokers. When someone politely asks you not to smoke you have three possible alternatives: you may put the cigarette out, go to a designated smoking area or tell him you have no intention of living to be an embittered old person. But thank him for his concern.

If a person is smoking on an elevator with you, remember that the ride will not last long. The smoker is breaking the law, but your contact with this person is on a short-term, one-shot basis. Unless you are very bothered by the smoke, it is best to let it pass and say nothing. If you are working closely with a smoker, tell him or her that the smoke bothers you and arrive at a compromise. Recent studies have shown that passive smoking, that is, inhaling someone else's smoke, does increase your risk of heart disease.

At lunch, request a table in the designated area for smoking. Do not start smoking until everyone at the table has finished eating. Try not to smoke between courses, but if you do, try to prevent smoke from going into another person's face. If you go to a restaurant with someone who does not smoke, and if you feel you can control your addiction, offer to sit in the nonsmoking section.

IT COULD COST YOU THE PRESIDENCY

Do you remember the 1960 televised debate between Richard Nixon and John Kennedy? That debate vividly revealed the importance of our visual image. From the beginning Kennedy had the advantage. He appeared more confident, stronger, more colorful, calmer, and more experienced. He looked taller, more dynamic and vigorous. His posture was open and erect and his hand gestures were coordinated with what he was saying. His note-taking made him appear more concerned and responsive. The viewing audience saw Kennedy as more dynamic and persuasive.

Nixon was rated as being weaker, unassertive, and nervous. As a result, he appeared less experienced and less knowledgeable. Nixon was slightly shorter than Kennedy and seemed tired and too thin. He stood on one leg occasionally and tightly griped the podium when speaking. He seemed unable to control unpleasant facial expressions. Nixon's dark beard, jowls, and the rings under his eyes gave Kennedy a distinct advantage.

Those who viewed the telecast voted Kennedy as the absolute, without-a-doubt winner of the debate. Ironically, those who listened to the debate on the radio declared Nixon as the distinct winner. He came across as the more experienced debater and was adept at specifically addressing the issues. Could it be that Nixon's physical appearance cost him the debate and the election?

Did your mother ever tell you that in America anyone can grow up and become the President of the United States of America . . . as long as you have the right visual image?

CHAPTER SIX

OFFICE DECOR

A FRIEND WHO worked for Admiral Rickover in the private sector said the Admiral was the master of the Power Office. The Admiral had his desk on a raised platform, two uncomfortable chairs were placed directly in front of his desk, and the chairs had the front legs shortened about two inches. When sitting in these chairs one would have to look up at the Admiral sitting behind his desk on a raised platform and lean forward because of the sawed-off chair legs. The visitor felt as if he had very little time to complete his business before being catapulted out of the chair. The sawed-off legs also made him crane his neck to look up to the elevated platform. The Admiral's desk was placed at the far end of his huge office. The visitor had to walk across all that space to get to the sawed-off chair and all the while the Admiral sat behind his desk glaring at him.

Kings, high priests, and many dictators have always known that the surroundings in which one works say a great deal about one. In the past the message communicated by most executive offices has been one of rank and authority. This seems to be changing to a more welcoming, living room decor or else to a relatively bare-bones alternative. The power office arrangement is giving way to an arrangement that enhances communication with others. Offices of middle managers often have couches and overstuffed chairs as well as a desk. The value of effective communication is breaking down the walls of the hierarchy.

Most office accoutrements are determined by rank. The location, size, number of windows and whether you get blinds or drapes is many times determined by rank. How many accessories you are allowed to have on your telephone, the quality and style of your office furniture and controllable access (is there a door to close?) are rank-dependent. The following are a few items that you do have control over.

A MESSY DESK IS A MESSY MIND

I saw a musical comedy some years ago entitled, "How to Succeed in Business Without Really Trying." The lead character was a young employee who was constantly trying to impress his boss, without really working. In one scene he arrived at work a few minutes before nine, and proceeded to loosen his shirt and tie, muss up his hair, fill ashtrays with cigarette butts, and throw papers and documents all over his office. When the boss arrived a few minutes later he found his employee "collapsed" at his desk, obviously comatose from working all night.

This ploy may work in some organizations that have a culture that believes, "An empty desk is an empty mind." But more often corporate cultures dictate that "A messy desk is a messy mind" and "An organized desk is an organized mind." Take a look at other peoples' desks; this corporate culture norm should become readily apparent.

Some people are afraid to clean up their desk because it might upset the ecology, others deliberately keep their desk piled high with paper so that the boss will think they are overworked. Most people pile papers everywhere because that reminds them of the unfinished work they must do. Nevertheless, if papers, books, office supplies, and personal items are placed where they belong, then you will not have to scramble around every time you need a particular item. Looking for needed documents creates anxiety and is a waste of time.

Having a clean desk is considerate for your visitors. A cluttered desk signals you have other work to do. Your clean desk signals that your visitor has your undivided attention. Your visitor will be more relaxed, comfortable, and in a better frame of mind to do business.

When you decide to go on an all-out spring cleaning of your desk, you should first schedule an appointment with yourself and write it on your calendar. When the date arrives, unplug your phone, close your door, and bring a large trash can. Give yourself two hours. Go through each pile one paper at a time. Ask yourself if each piece of paper is needed. If you decide it is no longer needed, throw it away. If it is important put it in the "keeper" pile. Sort every pile in your office—desk, bookshelf, windowsill.

Using a legal pad, make a list of all the papers you have left. This is an inventory of your unfinished work and ongoing projects. This is your ongoing master plan for keeping track of current and future projects.

Just cramming all the stuff on your desk into a few drawers will not help you when you need to retrieve those materials. You need an efficient filling system. Put all papers that deal with a client, customer or project in an individual manila folder. Label your files accordingly.

Organize your remaining desk drawers. Get rid of the junk

you've collected over the years. Keep things you use frequently in a handy location.

The only things that you should keep on your desk are a picture of your family, the project that you are presently working on and your daily "To Do" list. Studies show that your power of concentration increases by at least 25 percent when your current work is the only thing occupying your field of vision. So put your current elephant in the middle of your desk and keep it there until you're done. If your elephant is still kicking at the end of the day, leave him sitting in the middle of your desk (but make sure he's housebroken). This will save you at least fifteen minutes of startup time the following morning. Every morning your first task should be making a list of items you wish to accomplish that day. Making a list organizes your priorities and can be a good scapegoat. When the boss comes into your office and says, "Did you call that salesman like I asked you to?" you can hold up your "To Do" list and say, "I have it right here on my 'To Do' list."

To deal with all that paper that is delivered to your office each day, be guided by the maxim, "Every time you pick up a piece of paper, make a decision about it." You basically have only four options: throw it away, refer it to somebody else, act on it, or file it. When the mail comes, read it, and make a decision. If you don't do something about it then and there, it is likely to become part of the piles of paper that mysteriously accumulate.

As Victor Hugo so aptly said, "He who every morning plans the transactions of the day, and follows that plan, carries a thread that will guide him through the labyrinth of the most busy life. The orderly arrangement of his time is like a ray of light which darts itself through all his occupations. But where no plan is laid, where the disposal of time is surrendered merely to the chance of incidents, all things lie huddled together in one chaos, which admits of neither distribution nor review."

YOU ARE YOUR BACKDROP

The picture you put on the wall behind your desk is seen whenever anyone is across your desk talking to you. What you select should project what you want to reflect. Many managers put a picture of a ship in a storm. This reflects a hard charger who is apt to say, "Don't tell me about the storms, just bring in the ship." Decide on what character trait you want to project and choose your backdrop accordingly. You may want a bookcase with massive volumes for an intellectual image or an abstract painting for a more creative image. Be careful with "far out" backdrops (someone may realize you are weird) and "still lifes" (someone may realize you are a still life).

A clever political tactic is to find out what charities the boss supports. A framed poster supporting the charity would be a nice addition to your office. (See "Give to the United Way or I'll Fire You.")

There is a form of art that should be called "Corporate Art." This art contains no nudes, has subdued colors, makes no political statements and has a scene that can be readily identified (rather than interpreted). Some examples are: ducks flying across a placid pond, a country scene with a trickling brook, or a city skyline. Corporate Art is to the eyes what muzak is to the ears. It's mellow and not distracting. One doesn't really look at it, but you know it's there.

LOVE YOUR DOG

Keep a family picture on your desk. A nice warm picture of you and your family will soften the heart of the most callous boss or client. Your children's progress in school or Little League is always a good safe topic for conversation. Boredom, however, will quickly develop if this topic is held for too long.

If you do not have a family, take an adorable picture of your dog—or your neighbor's dog—and put it where the family picture belongs. The objective is to create an air of benevolence. The picture you choose should be of some person or animal that you love—or wish you had the opportunity to love. When you look at the picture it should elicit good feelings from you as well as from others that see the picture. When work gets hectic and you feel overwhelmed, take a glance at the picture for a little pick-me-up.

DOS UP THE PC AND GIVE IT THE BOOT

Many people have computerphobia. Some of these fears may have originated from George Orwell's *1984*. In this book, computers monitored everyone. Governmental controls were stifling. We know today that his predictions did not come true ... at least not entirely...

Others fear computers because they don't like or trust technology they do not understand. If this logic is carried to the extreme, most of these people would have to do without fire. Others fear computers because they may catch a computer virus from them or they cannot bring themselves to touch the mouse. Still others fear the computer may take their job. While working as a corporate trainer a software dealer tried to sell me a program that would teach a seminar that I taught... I did not buy the program. Like them, fear them or hate them, computers are here to stay. Those who resist the technology will be left in a cloud of dust.

My first book was written with a pencil, several hundred erasers, and a stack of legal pads. I could cut and paste by cutting out paragraphs and literally pasting them where I wanted. I could check my spelling by using a dictionary, and I could find the exact word I wanted by using a thesaurus. I could produce typed materials by taking the work to my typist. I could do everything a computer could do, so why should I buy a computer? In one word . . . SPEED! My first book, which is about the same length as this one, took almost two years to write, whereas this one took about six months. The quality may have also improved. The ease of changing and rearranging the material motivated me to do more editing. With a pencil, editing was so laborious that I may have let a few phrases stand as written that should have been rewritten.

A few hours after I wrote the above paragraph, my computer suddenly locked. I had not saved my material for several hours. I called a friend and asked her what I should do. She said, "The only thing you can do at this point is turn the computer off, but you will lose your last three hours of work." I take back some of the nice things I said about writing on a computer. I was able to remember most of what I had written but what if I had not been able to do that? What if the Great American Novel had been glitched out of existence? To err is human— but to really screw up requires a computer.

This horror story could have been prevented from happening. All I needed to do was save my material every fifteen minutes. That way when the inevitable glitch occurs, you lose only the last fifteen minutes of the material you have written. Excuse me while I go save this paragraph.

Try to have a personal computer in your office, even if you don't use it. A computer as office decor makes an impression that you are up to date, modern, attuned to the changing world. The computer doesn't have to work, you don't even have to plug it in; just let it sit there. If it creates the image you want, it's doing its job.

Of course it is a good idea to become computer literate. In the office, as opposed to the restroom, we are rapidly approaching the paperless society. The U.S. Postal Service may be cut back, as more and more of us use electronic mail. Fewer trees will be cut down to produce paper, and the speed of doing business will forever accelerate. To transact business in the year 2000 you will, at the minimum, need to become computer literate. Lotus 1–2–3 has nothing to do with sports cars or learning how to count to three.

> Remember the bookkeeper
> Perched on his stool,
> Green eye-shade tilted,
> Quill for a tool?
> He wasn't too fast,
> But nowhere in town
> Did you hear the excuse
> "Our computer is down."
>
> —R. S. SULLIVAN

SITTIN' & YAKKIN'

Most offices have a desk and three chairs. One chair is for you and the other two are for your visitors. Rather than have both chairs in front of your desk, put one chair in front and one on the side of the desk. For some conversations it is best not to have the desk separating you from your visitor. The conversation becomes more intimate when there is no desk between you.

DIPLOMAS

Upper-echelon executives within an organization tend to all be graduates of the same university. This is the old fraternity/ sorority system at its best. If you went to the same university, proudly display your diploma. If you went to an inferior or rival school, keep your diploma at home.

You may want to plan to send your children to the preferred school, and tell everyone about it.

HOLIDAYS

Some people have the Scrooge Syndrome; they feel that the office is no place for Christmas decorations. Others want to put garlands around the edge of each desk, tinsel hanging from the ceiling and holly in every window. Non-Christians may object, but such objections should be considered rude. It is impolite to expect others not to celebrate a holiday simply because you do not share their belief. If two holidays of different religions occur at approximately the same time, such as Hanukkah and Christmas, then decorations should be put up to commemorate both holidays.

Similarly, different racial groups may observe certain holidays in different ways. In a mixed office the Chinese New Year may be celebrated by some and Martin Luther King's birthday by others. All racial and spiritual traditions should be given equal consideration. It is extremely rude to observe one holiday or tradition and ignore the others in a mixed office.

MUSIC INFLAMES THE SAVAGE BOSS

Ten years ago, keeping a radio playing at one's desk was a definite no-no. Today, in some departments and for some positions, this taboo has loosened up a bit. In most art departments music can be heard trickling through the corporate corridors. Many secretaries play their radios while doing dull or repetitive tasks. In these cases the music helps to make the work more pleasant and may even help in productivity.

In most other professional areas one should not play one's radio while working. Listening to music while working may indicate to the boss that you are not concentrating and music may be distracting to visitors and coworkers. Everyone knows that rock & roll rots the soul and Muzak puts it to sleep.

CHAPTER SEVEN

BUSINESS POLITICS

The relation between superiors and inferiors is like that between wind and grass. The grass must bend when the wind blows over it.

—CONFUCIUS

BUSINESS POLITICS IS a game. It can be silly, superficial, cold, hard, and ruthless. It can also be interesting, alluring, and fun. If you decide to put your nose to the grindstone and ignore politics, you will not understand much of what is going on around you. Consider it as a game, with very high stakes, namely self-preservation. Who knows, you may come to enjoy it.

THE TRUE MEANING OF BUSINESS

You may think your job is to get work done, make a profit, or run a department. This is simply not so. Your job is to please your boss and his job is to please his boss and her job is to please her boss and the CEO has to please the Board of Directors and the Board of Directors must please the stockholders and finally the stockholders have to please their creditors. To please your boss you must do something that will make him look good to his boss. Each link in the chain of command exists to make the next link look better. A boss does not see you as a friend, he sees you as someone who will make him look good, or someone that will make him look bad. He doesn't want to hear about your personal problems—his only interest is how your performance will be affected and consequently, his.

The definition of a killer boss is "A person who takes all the credit, avoids all the work and shifts all the blame."

Military training will help you blend into many corporate cultures. You have to know when to say "Yes, sir," "I'm sorry, sir," "I'll do it your way, sir." Unless you learn very quickly how to bow to your boss, you never will be a boss yourself.

I CAN DO IT, GIVE IT TO ME

People who get the things done that make their bosses look good are promoted more rapidly than others. These people are usually independent self-starters. They grew up counting on themselves to find things to do, not on their parents, peers, or television.

Even if you were a whiner, there is still hope. These qualities can be developed later in life. All it takes is an "I can do it" attitude. A few suggestions:

- When given an assignment, react to it with enthusiasm, as if you are eager to do it. The worst thing you can do is roll your eyes up and expel a large amount of air in an audible sigh. Do every job you're assigned as if it were a job worth doing, even if it's grunt work. As Vince Lombardi said, "If you aren't fired with enthusiasm, you will be fired with enthusiasm."

- Never ask thoughtless questions when given an assignment. Ask yourself if you really need to ask the boss for the information or can you get it through some other source. Even if the boss says, "Don't be afraid to ask questions," make sure she means it. Employees who ask a lot of questions are often viewed as lacking initiative and overly dependent. At times it may be better to make a mistake than to ask thoughtless questions. People ask stupid questions for a reason.

- When you do make a mistake, 'fess up to it, don't try to blame somebody else, the market conditions, or God. Excuses will only make you appear defensive. It's better to say, "I made a mistake and I will do the following to correct it . . ."

  People who are insecure have the hardest time admitting their mistakes. They fail to realize that it is not the mistake itself but how a mistake is handled that forms the lasting impression.

- Never hurry through a job, hoping to impress your boss with your speed. Do the assignment with care and without haste. Rushing through an assignment may indicate to the boss that you have contempt for the work. People will forget how fast you did a job, but they will remember how well you did it. The faster you do your work, the less time you are spending proofreading, thinking, and planning. Never miss an opportunity to set a deadline for yourself. Then make sure you deliver on time and as promised.

- Don't run to your boss every time you have a problem. Try to work it out for yourself. After careful consideration, present the problem to your boss. Don't expect an immediate solution; after all, you are closer to the problem.
- Never turn down an assignment because you think it is beneath your talents.

If you take all of these suggestions and if you are fortunate enough to have a boss who is moving up, she may bring you with her. Upwardly mobile executives like to gather around them groups of young people who will support them.

THE ESSENTIAL RIGHT ARM

When you have a boss that is climbing up the corporate ladder, you should give him a strong right arm to help him in his quest. Do everything you can for him, work especially hard when he gives you an assignment no matter how small or insignificant, and be willing to work overtime when he asks you to go to Angola.

In order to catch the rising star, you should draw favorable attention to the star and to yourself. If someone gives you a compliment for a job well done, ask her to put it in writing. The letter may be addressed to your boss to highlight yourself, or even better, if what you did involved a departmental effort, the letter may be sent to your boss's boss. Remember, your job is to make your boss look good.

To be the boss's essential right arm, it's essential that you literally sit on your boss's right side during meetings. The best time to show up for meetings is to walk in right behind the boss. When discussions start, be on the right side of your boss's position. Never open your mouth in the meeting unless you have your facts right.

THE MOTHER HEN

Mother hens have been called mentors, rabbis, and godfathers; no matter what you call them their function remains the same. The mother hen is someone who takes you under her wing, protects you, guides you, and helps you develop. A mother hen is someone you respect and admire.

It's very difficult to move up to high places within an organization without a mentor. Dr. Harry Levinson of the Levinson Institute of Cambridge, Massachusetts says, "Why don't people make it without mentors? The reasons are simple. All organizations necessarily must be political. That is, they are made up of individuals and groups of people who need each other's help to get work done."

Unless you have the political clout of your mother hen standing behind you, it may be impossible for you to break into the organization's network, that is, the informal associations where most of the work is done. Without a mother hen clucking for you when positions open up, your chance of even being considered are slim.

Your mother hen may be your boss or some other influential person. They can be either in or outside of the organization. To find a mother hen, first look around the chicken coup and find a hen you admire, go to the hen and ask for guidance or counsel on a project. Make sure the project you pick is an interesting one and one that you know enough about so that you don't appear like a dumb chicken. If there are no admirable hens in your coop, try to find a hen in your field or profession outside your coop. Of course a hen outside your coop is not in the political pecking order as is the hen within the organization. Nevertheless, your coop isn't the only coop in the country; the outside hen may have friends in your coop, or can recommend you for positions that develop in the other coop.

USE YOUR NETWORK

Networking is being able to help or benefit from individuals you directly have a relationship with to achieve life's goals. As Cavett Robert says, "We can be walking encyclopedias of knowledge and yet go to the grave with music still within ourselves unless we can master the art of networking. With our changing values, shifting methods, and increasing competition, we find networking far more important than ever before. We must circulate if we expect to percolate. And we must make contacts if we expect to make contracts."

Keeping your networking skills sharply honed is an essential part of any career advancement strategy. Networking is not just going to parties and haphazardly giving and collecting business cards. In a new book, *Is Your Net Working?* (New York: Wiley, 1989) Anne Boe and Bettie Youngs define networking as an organized way of "linking" up with others to exchange information, advice, contacts and support. Keep your information about your contacts on a computer or notebook. List their names, addresses, phone numbers and a note about your encounter with the individual.

Find out to which organizations the individual belongs and whom they know. Most importantly, don't be shy to tell others that you are looking for information on job openings, pay scales, contracts, etc. Ask specifically for what you want or whether your contact knows anyone that may help you get what you want.

Keep an accurate record of the favors you do for others and the favors they do for you. After doing a favor for someone, it is perfectly acceptable to remind the individual what you did for him or her, when asking for a reciprocal favor. Networking is give and take and there should be a reasonable balance between the two. You can gauge how common reciprocity is by the number of clichés in our language expressing the same thought:

- You scratch my back, I'll scratch yours.
- What goes around comes around.
- You get what you give.
- When you live for others they will live for you.

Some resources for developing a network of connections are:

- Relatives—for all you know, Uncle Oley may know someone who can help you.
- Friends—all things being equal, people will buy from a friend. All things being not quite so equal, people will still buy from a friend.
- Neighbors—an over-the-fence chat can turn up helpful information.
- Old classmates—they should never be forgotten. Keep in touch with them.
- Business associates—some of your best information could come from people you work with, or have done work for.
- People you meet at conventions—often from different parts of the world, they can broaden your network considerably.
- Local associations—some of the strongest network connections come from organizations such as: National Speakers Association, the PTA, the Rotary Club, the American Society of Training and Development, and countless others. These relationships get stronger because you see each other frequently and for a common cause.
- Make a special effort at forming network relationships with those people whose work can affect yours.

The net is as wide as you want to make it, and the farther it's cast, the better your catch. Most people will be glad to help you, just as you will be happy to return the favor when you're in a position to help someone.

THE WORLD'S MOST DANGEROUS QUESTION

"Boss, can I have a raise?"

"The only raise you'll get out of me is my foot raised to the seat of your pants when I kick you out of the door—you're fired!"

"But boss, you can't fire me. I do the work of three people in this office."

"Yeah? Tell me who the other two are and I'll fire them too."

This exchange may sound outlandish, but nevertheless it happens. At most companies, asking for a raise is sheer insanity. It may get you fired and even if you succeed it stands to lower the opinion the boss has of you. Forever afterwards the employer will consider you disloyal; money is more important to you than the company. It is estimated that fewer than 5 percent of executives ask for a raise in any given year.

Companies tie their decisions on salary increases to the formal performance reviews. A problem arises when the boss does not do the appraisals. Many consider the reviews as unnecessary since they comment on your work frequently anyway. Others are afraid to confront subordinates about poor performance.

If you are given a performance review and you disagree with your rating, most companies will offer a formal appeals procedure. The appeal is usually made with your boss, who made the appraisal, his boss, who will invariably support your boss's opinion, and little old you. It is best not to dispute the review because you will never win. Most people feel that they are in the top 10 percent, but everyone can't be there. The most unfair and brutal reviews come from companies that require managers to evaluate their people so that the results fall within a bell-shaped curve. In this system 10 percent must be at the bottom; whether they deserve it or not.

If you insist on throwing precaution to the wind and foolishly asking for a raise, then use this four-part system:

1. Gather hard data on what you've accomplished for the company.
2. Time your request. Asking for a raise when the company is doing poorly or down-sizing is tantamount to career suicide. The best time, if there is a best time, is when you're assigned a new task with more responsibility. Ask whether this carries a commensurate increase in pay.
3. Put your request for a meeting to discuss your salary increase in writing. Never surprise your boss by just walking into his or her office and asking for a raise. Your memo should first express your loyalty to the company, list the goals that were set for you and list your accomplishments. With great tact, request your raise, and then reiterate your loyalty to the company.
4. When you have your meeting be humble. As the old country song goes, "Oh Lord, it's hard to be humble when you're perfect in every way."

Assure your boss you want to kick around the idea and that you don't expect an immediate decision. Then present your case. Never beg, whine or complain and most of all don't threaten. You probably still won't get the raise; the best you can hope for is a clear set of objectives for future performance that will earn you the raise. If you don't even get that, look for another job somewhere else. Nothing ventured nothing gained; you didn't like working for that cheap, slave-labor company anyway . . . did you?

If a head-hunter calls and says, "Hey Vern, this is your old buddy Ernest, and have I got a deal for you. The local gas company has an opening just like your job at the the electric company and is willing to pay you 10 percent more than your present salary." Suppose you have some interest, go to the interview and they make you an offer. What now?

If you have the job secured, but you would really prefer not working for the gas company, go to your boss and tell him about it, but emphasize the fact that you are a loyal employee. Instead of saying. "They've offered me 10 percent more, either match it or I'm out of here," say, "I feel a kinship to this company and I really like working here. What can the company do for me so I won't have to take this other job?"

GIVE TO THE UNITED WAY OR I'LL FIRE YOU

Many companies sponsor United Way drives. The CEO will usually make a speech or issue a memo encouraging employees to give something, even if they can't afford their fair share. The names of noncontributors are often given to the CEO. Contributing indicates that you are loyal, a team player, and have a good moral character. If you did not contribute you are cheap, disloyal, and stingy.

One of the best ways of getting visibility is to volunteer to spearhead the United Way drive in your company. Before volunteering for this position you should realize that your goal is to beat the record of the spearhead last year. This is not an easy position; you must distribute flyers, make speeches, and start the rumor that anyone not giving their fair share may be seen as a nonteam player. If you make the goal it's cheers and champagne; if you don't it's tears and embarrassment. It's a risky position, but if you are willing to give it 100 percent it may be worth it.

A CEO called one of his employees and said, "Our report shows that you made no contribution to the United Way this year. I pay you $50,000 a year and you can't afford a small donation?"

The employee asks, "Does your report also show that my mother has an incurable disease that will cost thousands of dollars in operations and hospital care if she is to recover?"

"No, it doesn't," the CEO admitted.

"Does it show that my brother was so badly wounded in the war that he refuses to return to America until certain plastic surgery can be completed and paid for?"

"No," said the CEO deeply moved. "How terrible to have one's family so affected."

"Does it show that my daughter's husband faces ruin unless he can raise money to pay for flood damage in his little shop?"

"No, it doesn't." The embarrassed CEO said, "I want you to know that I understand."

"I knew you would," the employee answered. "After all, if I am not giving any money to them, how can I justify contributing to the United Way?"

Dig down deep and give something, even if it hurts a little. You do not have to give your "fair share" to stay off the list. Besides, you either pay a little now or you may pay a lot later on.

Be careful about how you go about working for a charity. I was almost fired one time for doing a charitable act. A lady from the March of Dimes called me and asked if I would be willing to help in the March of Dimes drive. I said that I would, and asked what she wanted me to do. She said, "I want you to dive into a vat of Jello." It seems that people were willing to contribute to the March of Dimes if they could see an executive dive into a vat of Jello. I didn't back out, but I didn't tell my boss either. The fateful day arrived, so I dressed in my Uncle Sam costume left over from Mardi Gras, and went to the gathering. There were hundreds of people in the auditorium, a four-foot deep pool of Jello, and a slide.

As I climbed the ladder, I was introduced: "This is Mr.

Vernon Crawford, Corporate Manager of Training and Development for (company name) Corporation." As I slid down the slide, I was blinded by the flash bulbs snapping pictures. The slide was not a high one, but with the flash bulbs flashing the trip seemed to take forever. I hit the Jello and realized something that I hadn't considered before the dive . . . Jello is cold. I got out of the pool promptly, a couple of coeds hosed me down to get the Jello off, and I thought the whole incident was over.

The next day my picture was blown up on the cover of the living section of the local newspaper. There I was in my Uncle Sam costume on the slide, just when I hit the Jello. The caption read, "(company name) Executive Takes a Slide." My boss was not pleased. He felt that I made a fool of myself and had implicated the company. It took me many years to live this down and even to this day, people ask: "Aren't you the guy that slid into the Jello?" Remember, do what you can for a charity without making a splash.

DON'T BE LATE

> *Men count up the faults of those who keep them waiting.*
>
> —FRENCH PROVERB

Most organizations have a deep-seated, almost compulsive need for time discipline, a need that seems to go beyond economic necessity. Edward T. Hall in his book, *Dances of Life: The Other Dimension of Time* (New York: Anchor Press/ Doubleday; 1983) says, "Time talks. It speaks more plainly than words. The message it conveys comes through loud and clear. Because it is manipulated less consciously, it is subject to less distortion than the spoken language. It can shout the truth where words lie . . ."

It has been said, "Punctuality is the courtesy of Kings." Being late is discourteous to those left waiting. People who are on time generally resent the fact that a coworker is late.

If a coworker's tardiness or early departures do cause problems for you, it is appropriate to discuss this problem with the untimely person. Then give him or her a week to change. If there is no change, then you should make a complaint to the boss. The boss may need the complaint to have a basis for a reprimand. Secretary to boss: "Certainly I have a good reason for being late everyday. It makes the workday seem much shorter."

Be on time every morning, take only sixty minutes for lunch and it is best to stay fifteen minutes overtime every day whether you need to or not. It has been said, "Time is money," but don't expect overtime for the fifteen minutes.

Time is not as urgent for some people as it is for others. A man taking a drive in the country happened upon a farmer feeding his pig in the most unusual manner. The farmer would lift his pig in his arms, hold it up to the branches of a tree and wait while the animal ate an apple. He would then move the pig from one apple to another . . . The city man watched this procedure for some time, then finally said to the farmer, "This seems an inefficient way of feeding your pig. Why don't you simply shake the apples off the tree and let the pig eat them from the ground? That would sure save a lot of time." The farmer looked puzzled, then shrugged and said, "What's time to a pig?"

AFTER WORK (5:15)

Does everyone head for the nearest bar after work and quaff down a few pints? I am not suggesting that you follow their example, but you could drop in occasionally and say hello. Never refuse to have a drink with the gang, even if it's only a club soda. Does everyone head for the health spa or running track? These activities may be healthier, and you should participate if you can, but they are less tasty and less filling.

SEXIST COMMENTS

In today's litigious world, every suggestive action, word or comment is a potential lawsuit. Writers are no longer free to use the universal "him." The replacements for "him" are : person, people, and him/her. Mailmen become mail carriers, firemen become fire fighters, and policemen become police officers. Sacramento sponsored a contest to find another name for the "manhole cover." One newspaper headline said the city was "Blowing the lid off sexist 'manholes,'" while another proclaimed that a "Tempest in a Manhole Sweeps City." Suggestions such as: person entry, exit port, personhole and innumerable others were submitted. The city counsel made the decision to call them maintenance hole covers. The public service did not need to change the MHC designation on the city maps. Hamilton, New Zealand—Sacramento's sister city—also held a renaming contest in which "sewer viewer" captured the top prize. There are so many words in the English language containing the word "man" that it would be chaos to make our language completely nonsexist.

A college professor's class was being picketed by a women's liberation group because the professor used sexist language in his classroom. The angry picketers were threatening to shut down his class completely until the professor brought them into the classroom and tried to defuse the tense situation. He admitted that he used sexist language and was trying to make amends and rid his speech of any taint of sexism. "Therefore," he told the class, "in this class we will now use 'neut' to refer to any male reference. For example: 'chairperson' will now be 'chairperneut,' 'manifest' will now be 'neutifest,' 'history' will now be 'neutory,' 'Thomas Jefferson' will now be 'Thomas

Jefferneut,' 'gentlemen' will now be 'neutleneuts,' 'ladies' will now be 'neuties.' "

A survey taken by the U.S. Merit Systems Protection Board found: "Forty-two percent of women and fourteen percent of men reported they had experienced sexual harassment." The board noted that victims are most often harassed by coworkers of the opposite sex. Twenty-two percent of the male victims, however, reported they were harassed by one or more men. The most frequently experienced type of uninvited attention is "unwanted sexual teasing, remarks, questions, and jokes."

Sexist remarks commonly take the form of such comments as:

"Anything you want, honey, I'm at your service."

"Hey Honeybuns, how about getting your old boss a cup of coffee."

"I'll have the report on your desk tomorrow; I could never say no to a hunk like you."

"Good morning, Sweet Pea, you look marvelous, simply marvelous."

Remarks such as these are not *intended* to harass, but the victim may *perceive* them as harassment. Determination of whether behavior is sexually harassing is not based on how it was intended, but on how it was received. The moral is: keep your mind on the bottom line and not on the bottom of your co-workers.

OXYMORON = COMPANY PARTY

He that makes himself an ass must not take it ill if men ride him.

—THOMAS FULLER, M.D.

The company party is not the time for letting your hair down, sowing wild oats or wearing the proverbial lamp shade. It is a time to talk about noncontroversial issues such as the weather, sports, movies, or food. Stay away from religion, politics and the company. You are not there to have a good time or to get wild and crazy. You should act as you would in the office.

This is the time to wear conservative party clothing. Keep a low profile; this is one time you do not want high visibility. My wife made a party dress for a New Year's Eve company party. This was our first company party, and we had no book telling us to wear conservative party clothing. The dress had a red satin top with a low front and back. The bottom was black satin, ruffled and short. We arrived at the dinner party and everyone, men and women, were dressed in blue or gray suits. Instead of good cheer, she was given a big serving of embarrassment.

Alcohol is usually the catalyst that gets you in trouble. It is not a fantasy—people do get drunk at company parties, tell their boss what they really think of them, and do, sometimes, get fired on the spot by their equally inebriated boss. Often the conflict is resolved on Monday morning, but the relationship remains tainted.

Alcohol also lowers our inhibitions about making sexual advances. The female executive wearing a conservative party dress, with a touch of perfume, may appear entirely different through an alcoholic haze than when she is in a business suit at the office. There is a double standard. To quote a female executive who suffers the scar to prove what she is saying, "Few people think badly of a man who gets drunk, but if a woman gets drunk it gets blown out of proportion. You see a woman dancing with an executive and everyone thinks she's having an affair with him—he isn't having one with her; she's having one with him." Women should be cautious, and men should be gentlemen and fully aware of the laws regarding sexual harassment.

The best advice is to dress appropriately, arrive on time,

and do not stay late. The longer you stay, the crazier it gets. Make sure everyone knows you made an appearance and then get out of there. You may then go to the nearest pub for whooping it up and/or crying in your beer.

An old Jewish proverb says, "The innkeeper loves the drunkard, but not for a son-in-law."

SHOULD I WEAR MY COAT?

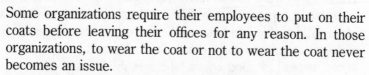

Some organizations require their employees to put on their coats before leaving their offices for any reason. In those organizations, to wear the coat or not to wear the coat never becomes an issue.

In most organizations the rule of thumb is: you do not wear your coat for a working meeting unless someone one rung above your boss is attending. Wear your coat to all formal addresses given by upper management. Wear your coat if you are making a presentation. The temperature has nothing to do with the decision.

POLITICS MAKES AN EMPTY BED

Keep your political affiliations to yourself, particularly if you are in variance with the organization. The same is true for religion.

While making a campaign speech, a candidate was trying to discover the dominant religion of his audience and he began by saying, "My great grandfather was an Episcopalian." There was stony silence. "But," he continued, "my great grandmother belonged to the Congregational church."

Again, silence. "My grandfather was a Baptist," more silence, "while my grandmother was a Presbyterian," still nothing. "But I had a great aunt who was a Methodist." "Yeah!"

followed by loud applause. "And I have always followed my great aunt," sustained cheering. The man was elected.

THE BUDGET, USE IT OR LOSE IT

If you have been allowed a certain amount during the fiscal year, USE IT! If you go under budget, you will be expected to spend only the smaller amount thereafter. Try to spend the *exact* amount in your budget; you will be considered a good estimator and provider of budgeted services. Remember: A penny saved is a penny lost in next year's budget.

SECRETARIAL ABUSE

The tasks of a secretary involve business only, not personal chores. A secretary should do your typing and filing, book appointments, make travel plans, and carry messages and memos to others. He or she should not be expected to wait on you or perform services such as bringing you coffee, typing personal correspondence, or lying about your whereabouts.

The secretary may, of course, answer your phone. It is best to answer your own phone. The caller doesn't waste time going through your secretary and a warmer communication with the caller may result. If you choose to have your calls screened to protect you from unwanted callers, don't ask your secretary to lie for you. He or she should simply say that you cannot take the call right now.

Many offices have one secretary shared among as many as six workers. When this is the case it is particularly important that you not waste the secretary's time. The boss in this situation who says, "Desirée, would you go get me a cup of coffee," is likely to incur the resentment of the secretary and the other subordinates sharing her services.

THIS COMPANY IS A NO-GOOD @#$%^&*!

Bad-mouthing the company will get you nowhere, except perhaps to the unemployment line. As old fashioned as it sounds, employers still want loyalty. If management hears you talking negatively about the company they may think you are looking for another job, driving away customers, or even worse, a union organizer.

Not only should you avoid saying bad things about your company, you should also refrain from saying anything bad about your coworkers and especially management. This is an "I'll scratch your back if you'll scratch mine" society. If you knife someone in the back, expect retribution.

A truck driver stopped at a roadside diner to eat. He got a hot dog, a bag of potato chips, and a Coke. As he was about to start eating, three rough-looking guys in leather jackets pulled up on motorcycles and came inside. One grabbed his hot dog and ate it. The second one drank his Coke, and the third one took his potato chips. The truck driver didn't say a word. He got up, paid the cashier, and went out the door. One of the bikers said to the cashier, "He ain't much of a man is he?" She said, "He's not much of a driver either. He just ran over three motorcycles."

If you really need to ventilate your feelings about the company, go to a private therapist.

COMPLIMENTS AND COMPLAINTS

There is an art to sincerely paying someone a compliment. Do it wrong and the compliment appears as a shallow form of flattery, or even worse, obsequiousness. Do it right and the person complimented is sure to remember what you have said and will invariably think better of you.

Some compliments are simple, telling someone you like his or her tie or purse is not a hard thing to do. This type of compliment should be done simply and briefly. If you overdo the amount or length of the compliment, the power to impress will wear thin. These compliments cost you nothing but may give the person being complimented a little ego boost.

Other, more serious compliments take a bit more planning and forethought. For example, after a CEO makes an after-dinner speech, many people are likely to tell her how dynamic she was, how they liked the introductory joke, or how impressed they were with the speech in general. With a bit more forethought one might say, "I've been giving a lot of thought to the comments you made about closing out the Beaver Falls plant. Your point about selling the plant to support our other loss leaders was very interesting. I would really like to talk to you about that sometime." With this compliment, you have shown that you truly listened and understood the speech.

Some management theorists think that when criticizing an employee, one should sandwich the criticism between compliments. For example, start the discussion by pointing out what the employee is doing right and complimenting that aspect of his work. Next, gently shift the focus of the discussion to the area that needs correction. Calmly suggest a better way to do the task. End the conversation with a friendly word, a pat on the back or some other signal indicating that the employee is still a respected member of the team.

The sandwich technique leaves the employee with a better understanding of the problem and a feeling that he has not been chastised but helped. As Mark Twain said, "I think a compliment ought to always precede a complaint, where one is possible, because it softens resentments and insures for the complaint a courteous and gentle reception."

THE CUSTOMER IS ALWAYS RIGHT

*Discussion is an exchange of knowledge; argument is
an exchange of ignorance.*

—ROBERT QUILLEN

Nothing is ever gained by winning an argument and losing a
customer. Giving the advice to stay calm when confronted by
an angry customer would be fine, except for the fact that for
some reason, anger makes your mouth work faster than your
mind.

Often, the difference between success and failure for an
individual or entire organization depends on the quality of customer service they provide. In many cases, the products are
basically the same and the prices are competitive. The ultimate
determining factor is how the customer is treated by those
serving him or her.

A typical business does not hear from 96 percent of its
dissatisfied customers. They just go away and 91 percent will
never come back. A survey of why customers quit doing business with a given concern indicated that 68 percent quit because of indifference toward the customer by the owner,
manager or some employee. They either had an argument
with someone in the company that was unsatisfactorily resolved or they couldn't find someone interested enough to help
them resolve their complaint. Seven out of ten complaining
customers will do business with you again if you resolve the
complaint in their favor. If you resolve it immediately, 95 percent will do business with you again. The typical dissatisfied
customer will tell eight to ten people about his problem.

To avoid or resolve arguments one must:

- Listen attentively to the customer without interrupting,
  ask questions to clarify the customer's needs, and em-

pathize with the customer's position. Signify to the customer that you are listening.

- Use simple, understandable words and explain technical matters in terms that the customer can understand. Repeat important or confusing information and demonstrate by using examples. Ask the customer for feedback to make sure the customer has understood. Encourage the customer to ask questions and be sensitive to body language ... your own and the customer's.

- Greet customers with a smile and use the customer's name if you know it. Introduce yourself and try to chat a bit with her before getting down to her complaint.

- Take a few deep breaths, bite your tongue and try to stay calm or at least make the appearance of being calm. Don't be personally offended by the customer's anger or outrage. Remember, the customer is not mad at you personally; they are mad at the product. Control yourself: remember that anger is only one letter short of danger.

- Sympathize with the customer to defuse anger. Investigate to find the root cause of the customer's complaint. If you're in the wrong, admit it. If you are willing to admit you are wrong, you're right. Negotiate a resolution to the customer's satisfaction. If the customer becomes overly irate or the resolution is beyond your control, ask for assistance.

Remember, the more hot arguments you win, the fewer warm customers you will have.

THE BOSS IS ALWAYS RIGHT

Many of the helpful hints in the above section also apply to this section. Most corporate types never see a customer: their work is done internally, insulated from customer contact. Arguments with customers for these people are not an issue; the boss is the point of contention.

Having an argument with your boss can have the same deleterious effect as having an argument with a customer... perhaps even more so. If you do emerge from a conflict victoriously, don't boast about your success.

Instead, stress how things worked out for the good of the department, which is a common goal. Just as you do not want to be reprimanded by your boss in front of others, neither does your boss want to argue with you (and especially lose) in front of others. If you must have an argument with your boss, ask to talk with her in her office. After the argument is over, tell your boss that you did not enjoy the conflict and that you are glad to be back working on the same side again. The scars will be slow to heal, and you will probably be regarded as a hot-head, so ask yourself, *Is the issue you are so hot about worth it?*

If you lose the argument you can always go over your boss's head and present the issue to your boss's boss. If this gets you what you want, it will mean that the higher boss has moved down into the position of your boss, as if your boss wasn't there at all. There is no greater enemy in the corporate world than the by-passed supervisor. You've managed to get him treated as if he didn't exist!

Sayings in the Bible are very often proved out in business. For example, tell the boss what you think of him—and the truth will set you free.

GIFT GIVING

The excellence of a gift lies in its appropriateness rather than in its value.

—CHARLES DUDLEY WARNER

Not only is it more blessed to give than to receive . . . it is also tax deductible. By law, gifts given to people outside the company are deductible business expenses only if they cost no more than $25. Gift giving can help cement a new business relationship or regenerate an old relationship, and it creates considerable goodwill. If the gift is inappropriate or given in a humdrum manner, it may annoy the recipient and even create problems.

In this litigious world, many people are reluctant to take a gift for fear of being accused of accepting a bribe. In business giving it's the thought that counts more than the cost. A gift too lavish can cause more embarrassment than one too modest. It may smack of payola or burden the recipient with an unwanted obligation.

During my ten years of business travel, I found one present that was appreciated by all, both nationally and internationally. A nice pen with the company's logo had universal appeal. Everyone writes. You don't know if they drink, smoke or read books.

Pens are small, light, and portable. A visitor does not want to lug home a heavy gift and you certainly don't want to bring a bulky, heavy gift on an airplane. Pens are used daily and each time the recipient uses the pen he is reminded of you. Pens are useful, practical and do not burden the recipient with an unwanted obligation. According to Incentive Marketing's survey, the top choices for gifts were, in declining order of popularity, pens or pen sets, clocks, liquor, calendars, diaries, watches, knives, fruit, glassware, jackets, and desk sets.

Pens are not appropriate if you know someone well. In this case you should give them something more personal that you know they will like. When someone is ill, a plant is appropriate; for celebrations send flowers.

Gifts should be given after a visitor has made a presentation for your company, when you visit another company and especially when you visit a company in another country. They may be sent or presented to someone to say "thank you" for a favor, to encourage someone starting a new job, when there is a death in the family, or to congratulate someone for just about anything.

Gifts should be given to your secretary for being effective and efficient in his or her job. The occasions for giving these gifts are birthdays, secretaries' week, and Christmas. When giving these gifts make sure that it is understood that there is no expectation of reciprocation. Your gift is to express thanks for a job well done, not to commemorate the given holiday.

As the secretary said to the boss, "For Christmas lets give each other sensible gifts . . . like ties and fur coats."

A gift costing between twenty-five and fifty dollars is appropriate: more than that is being too generous and may cause the secretary to feel the need to reciprocate. The gift may be such things as an article of clothing (but not undergarments), a gift certificate or a piece of nice pottery. Birthdays are best remembered with flowers or some fine chocolates. It is also nice to bring back a small gift when returning from a business trip to a foreign country.

The secretary may feel some need for reciprocation. If so, the gift should be some small token costing about ten dollars. An appointment book, wallet or wearable accessory is acceptable. The gift the boss gives to the secretary is given for some special service. Since the boss does not serve the secretary, reciprocal gifts are not necessary.

As Winston Churchill said, "It is better to have the power to give than to receive."

THE COMPANY NEWSLETTER

Does your company have a newsletter? If so, newsletters can be a great source of visibility within the company. I used the newsletter to its best advantage at every opportunity. The first step is to make friends with the company photographer. With the photographer firmly on your side, you can call him for any newsworthy event in which you happen to be involved. It doesn't have to be an earth-shaking event to get into the newsletter; the writers are usually willing to take anything just to fill up space. I became known as the most photographed employee in the company's history.

I would call the photographer after every seminar I taught; my picture as well as a group shot of the attendees appeared in the paper. This gave me visibility and made the seminar seem more important to the attendees.

I entered every contest the company sponsored, and tried hard to win. If I won, there was my picture. If I didn't win I still managed to get in the background when the picture of the winner was taken. My theory was, if I didn't win, at least I could be seen in the company of winners.

At company-sponsored sports events, the photographer, because he was my friend, would single me out when he was covering the event. He always took great action shots such as: Vern making a home run, Vern spiking the volleyball, and Vern crossing the finishing line in the Corporate Cup.

In playing this visibility game, you must be certain that the picture that appears shows you in a favorable light. A friend of mine was photographed while eating lunch. There was a beer bottle in front of his plate, and he was about to put a huge chunk of food into his mouth. They blew the picture up so that this scene made up the entire cover of the newsletter, along with the caption, "The New Orleans Lunch." This newsletter was sent to all company locations, including some Arab countries, where alcohol is forbidden. My friend's career never progressed after this photo appeared, in fact, he was "laid-off" soon afterwards. No reference was made to the photograph during his exit interview, but the feeling was there.

Remember, all visibility is not necessarily good visibility. (Also see "Give to the United Way or I'll Fire You.")

CHAPTER EIGHT

COMMUNICATIONS

WHY WRITE?

THERE IS A time to write and a time to speak and a time to do both. If you choose the wrong medium your message may be misunderstood. The criteria for choosing oral versus written communications is best understood in terms of four considerations: feedback, documentation, contacting large numbers of people, and the chain of command.

With oral communication you get immediate feedback. When ideas or statements are unclear, the receiver of the information can readily ask for clarification. Written communication must stand on its own for a longer period of time. Weeks may pass before an opportunity to clarify a point presents itself. If you need to be understood quickly or if the topic is vague or difficult to convey, there is no substitute for ear-to-ear communication.

The primary reason to put it in writing is for documentation. When you need to convey a complex set of facts or figures, write them down. As Confucius said, "A poor handwriting is better than a good memory." Facts and figures are easily forgotten, distorted, and even purposely manipulated unless they are written down. An employee's or coworker's memory can be easily refreshed when you have written material to support your points. As Dean Acheson said, "A memorandum is written to protect the writer, not to inform his reader."

When you need to communicate to a large number of people, you have two choices: call them all together or send a memo. Calling them all together is your most expensive option. If you need to reach thousands of people, you would have to rent a large auditorium, pay for travel cost, and you would have to give them a handout anyway. With the advent of copying and fax machines, large numbers of people can be reached very quickly. Additionally, written materials ensure uniformity of the information received. Some individuals are better listeners than others and the data they perceive may vary radically when there is no permanent, written record. Think of the confusion if price changes were conveyed to a thousand different buyers without the assistance of a price list.

It is best to use written communications when information must be passed down a chain of command, especially when there are many levels of authority. Due to differing interpretations of words and frames of reference, and short memories, oral communications are frequently distorted, as illustrated in the following story.

A Colonel issued the following verbal directive to the Executive Officer: "Tomorrow evening at approximately 2000 hours Halley's Comet will be visible in this area, an event that occurs only once every seventy-five years. Have men fall out in the battalion area in fatigues, and I will explain this rare phenomenon to them. In case of rain, we will not be able to see anything, so assemble the men in the theater and I will show films of it."

The Executive Officer told the Company Commander: "By order of the Colonel, tomorrow at 2000 hours Halley's Comet will appear above the battalion area. If it rains, fall the men out in fatigues; then march to the theater where the rare phenomenon will take place, something that happens every seventy-five years."

Company Commander to Lieutenant: "By order of the Colonel in fatigues at 2000 hours tomorrow evening, the phenomenal Halley's Comet will appear at the theater. In case of rain in the battalion area, the Colonel will give another order, something that occurs every seventy-five years."

Lieutenant to Sergeant: "Tomorrow at 2000 hours the Colonel will appear in the theater with Halley's Comet, something that happens every seventy-five years. If it rains, the Colonel will order the comet into the battalion area."

Sergeant to Squad: "When it rains tomorrow at 2000 hours the phenomenal seventy-five-year-old General Halley, accompanied by the Colonel, will drive through the battalion area in his fatigues."

RULES FOR INTERNAL MEMORANDA

After careful consideration you've decided that the information that you want to communicate fits into one of the above three categories. When composing your memo keep in mind the following points:

- Always begin with "To," "From," the date, and a one-word or one-sentence description of the subject of your correspondence.
- The first paragraph should state the point you want to make. Don't give a series of facts or figures and then dramatically state your point. State your point first and then give supporting documentation.
- A memo over one page is too long. When you go over one page you are probably discussing information, or giv-

ing an opinion. Discussions should be held face-to-face or over the phone. Memos should not be used for discussions; they should be used only to pass on information.

- Wait at least twenty four hours before sending any type of controversial memo or a memo written in an angry state of mind. (See "There's No Remittin'.")
- Proofread, proofread, proofread.

TYOPS ARE AN OHNO!

Typos and misspellings will kill the most well-planned proposal. The reader that catches the error will consider the proposal as slapped together in a slipshod way. As the sign on the boss's bulletin board says: TO ERR IS HUMAN, TO FORGIVE IS NOT COMPANY POLICY.

Dan Quayle gets slapped around by the press often enough without having made a mistake on his Christmas cards. A misspelling of "beacon" was contained in a holiday message handwritten by the vice president's wife, Marilyn Quayle, who has a law degree from Indiana University. Her staff and the printer failed to catch the error. The card read, "May our nation continue to be the bea*k*on of hope to the world." It is signed, "Fondly, the Quayles." The error appeared on 30,000 cards mailed at the expense of the Republican National Committee from Quayle's Indianapolis office. Poor Dan gets criticized for being too young for his office; now they are saying he can't spell, either.

A typo on the society page of a Chicago newspaper read, "Following the wedding the deception began." This paper used to have so many typographical errors that an irate reader once wrote to the managing editor: "Don't change a thing in your composing room, I've just broken your code."

Many writers try to pepper their writing with sophisticated sounding foreign words. If you positively must use a foreign word or phrase, make sure the spelling is correct.

One New Orleans uptown restaurant catering to the yuppie crowd literally sprinkled their menu with misspelled foreign words: hord'derves for *hors d'oeuvres*, cordon blue for *cordon bleu*, their French dip sandwiches were "with *au jus* on the side," and the salad dressing was au naturale instead of *au naturel*. As a favor to the restaurant owner I pointed out these misspellings and her response was, "Nobody's noticed this before, and besides it costs too much to reprint the menus."

An ad in the local paper read, "Four boneified bird dog puppies for sale." The word is "bonafide" and should not be confused with what the dogs eat.

In San José, California, red-faced administrators have ordered workers to tear down a huge multilingual welcome banner outside The San José Public Library after several Philippine patrons complained that in Tagalog the greeting actually meant "circumcision." The $10,000 banner, which took a San Francisco sign company three months to complete, was supposed to be a centerpiece decoration for a rededication ceremony. Scores of city leaders were scheduled to help rename the library after civil rights leader Martin Luther King, Jr. Other "welcomes" later turned out to be wrong; the Swedish and Dutch greetings were misspelled. More than one person wondered: how could this happen at a library? No one took responsibility for the errors.

SENIOR PARTNER: That new stenographer spells ridiculously.

JUNIOR PARTNER: Does she? Well, if she does, that's about the only word she knows how to spell.

Some general observations about typos:

• Success in finding typos is in inverse proportion to the finder's income.

- Typos appear in inverse proportion to the number of syllables in the misspelled word.
- The number of typos missed will increase in direct proportion to the number of people who will see the copy.
- Typos will be found only after the final copies have been reproduced, bound, and mailed.

A good way to catch typos is to read your material backwards. In this way your eyes will not skip over individual words in phrases. Chow waht I maen?

GET THE NAME RIGHT

When you misspell someone's name on a piece of office correspondence, the addressee may question the accuracy of other information in the letter, and may also get the impression that you:

- Did not care enough to get his name right
- Are sloppy in your business dealings
- Mailed the letter to the wrong person

A well-known author submitted an article to the editor of a business journal. He had two other articles published in this journal and anticipated no problems in getting his new article published. Within a week of mailing the article the author received a rejection letter. The P.S. on the rejection letter provided a clue as to why his article was rejected:

> I know the spelling of my last name is rather untraditional, but it has suited me and my family for seven generations. The name is Mackye not Mackey! You got it right twice before. How come you could not get it right this time?

The use of "Ms." is in such common use that there is little discussion anymore on the propriety of its use. At work a woman is herself, not her husband's wife. If someone objects, make a note of it so you can address her as she chooses. Most objections come from the older generation. If a woman writes to you with the prefix "Mrs.", then you should always address communications to her in the same manner.

When someone writes to you with a professional designation after his name, then you should return in kind. When you use a professional title do not also use a prefix. Use "Harriett A. Handshaw, R.N." not "Ms. Harriett A. Handshaw, R.N."

In another situation, a salesperson was trying to get a new account with the buyer of a large manufacturing concern. On a sales introduction letter, she addressed a "Ms. Shannon Sharp" as "Mr. Shannon Sharp." Ms. Sharp did not even dignify the salesperson with a reply.

Much to my displeasure, research proves professors give higher scores to papers thought to be submitted by men, which handicaps a boy named Sue, not to mention the thousands of women named Sue. Temma Kaplan, director of the Bernard Center for Research on Women says, "Because a teacher's expectation of success strongly influences a child's performance, I support gender-neutral names. A boy's name is especially helpful for women entering a male-dominated profession like engineering, architecture, and other hard sciences, though it certainly won't guarantee success."

Many parents name their children after movie stars. They may choose from names like Glenn Close, Sean Young, and Daryl Hannah. Giving a daughter a name like Whoopie or Peggy-Sue could be a handicap if she wanted to become a CEO of U.S. Steel. Some women are even dropping their first and middle names and just using initials.

Always check the spelling, sex, prefix, and title before sending a letter of any kind. Few things are more important to an individual than his own name. It is central to his identity.

PLURALS

The rules when forming plurals are full of exceptions. It is very hard to pin down when one uses "s," "es," or "ies." The following rules may prove useful:

THE PLURAL GUIDE

If the noun ends in "o" when preceded by a vowel, always add an "s," when preceded by a consonant, usually add an "es," but musical terms ending in "o" add only "s" and there are other words ending in "o" where you add only "s." Nouns ending in "s," " x," " ch," and "z" add "es." For nouns ending in "y" preceded by a consonant, change the "y" to "i" and add "es"; when preceded by a vowel, simply add "s." For nouns ending in "ful," add an "s" to the end of the word.

Now let's address Greek and Latin plurals: we have one curriculum, and two curricula. One criterion, and two criteria. One phenomenon, and two phenomena. One male alumnus, two male alumni, one female alumna, two female alumnae. A guest speaker's fee is an honorarium; congressmen and other speakers receive honoraria. One datum, two data. On "Star Trek: The Next Generation," the android named Commander Data should be Commander Datum, since there is only one of him, or . . . it?

You may want to make a copy of "The Plural Guide" and have it laminated. Carry it in your wallet or purse at all times. You will never again be perplexed by plurals. You may want to make several copies and give them to your friendes.

The question of the correct plural of the word "mongoose" was solved by a gentleman who wanted a pair of these interesting and affectionate creatures. He wrote to a dealer: "Sir, please send two mongeese." He did not like the look of this, tore up the paper, and began again: "Sir, please send two mongooses." This version did not satisfy him any better than the first, so he wrote: "Sir, please send me a mongoose, and, by the way, send me another."

I'M CONCERNED ABOUT...

Kindness in words creates confidence.

LAO-TZU

Rarely in the business world do you read a memo saying, "I'm mad as hell and you had better do something about it." Usually the tone is softened to say, "I'm concerned about... and I would appreciate your giving it your immediate attention." In order to really understand what is being communicated you must read between the lines. See if you can determine what's really being communicated in the following sentence:

Because of our negative cash flow position we are forced to curtail redundancies in the human resources area.

This sentence actually means, "Because we are broke, we have to fire people." Try another sentence:

The economically disadvantaged live in substandard housing units in the inner cities.

This sentence means, "Poor people live in slums."

You are being impacted by job discontinuance and reassigned for outplacement consultation.

"You're fired."

The following is the dictum of Edward Frank Allen, the hard-boiled editor of a well-known newspaper, to his reporters:

> We do not commence. We begin. We do not purchase. We buy. We do not pass away. We die. We are not all gentlemen but we are all men. Not all women are ladies, but all women are women. We do not reside in residences. We live in homes. We do not retire. We go to bed. Our priests, ministers and rabbis are not divines. Our lawyers are not barristers. Our undertakers are not morticians. Our realtors are not real estate dealers. Our plumbers are not sanitary engineers. Our cobblers are not shoe rebuilders. And the first reporter who writes about a body landing "with a dull sickening thud" will land with a dull sickening thud on the street, with hat in one hand and pay envelope in the other.

Euphemisms will usually not get you fired, but they should be used sparingly.

The federal government has a language of its own. For example: "unemancipated minors" stands for teenagers, "measurable in products" for results, "technology transfer assistance" for giving advice, and "effective linkages" for coordinating. It seems as if the government is trying to match the inflation in the economy with their inflated language.

Another common practice in writing business communications consists of eliminating all unnecessary verbiage, using few descriptive adjectives and avoiding all personal references. This results in a stiff and sterile message devoid of warmth and personality. Such communications create the impression that the writer is uncaring, distant, cold or blunt.

To change your missiles into memos with warmth, imagine the facial expressions and emotional responses of the memo's recipient. Try to relax while you are writing and close your letters with, "My best regards" instead of "Sincerely."

ONCE WRITTEN THERE'S NO REMITTIN'

There is a good reason for the sterile, watered-down prose of business writing... once written there is no taking it back. Have you ever gotten really angry at a significant other and written a scorcher of a letter to her, only to wish you hadn't the moment you dropped it in the mailbox? These impulsive, angry communications are better left unwritten. If you feel an urgent need to write your feelings down on paper, then do so, but sit on the letter or memo for a few days until you calm down. Make sure you hide the document during your cooling off period.

Bryant Gumble vented his hostile feelings about Gene Shalit and Willard Scott in a memo that he did not mail. Someone found it in his computer and made it public knowledge. Reports of the memo were broadcast on TV, radio, and newspapers across the country. His reputation as "Mr. Nasty" was reinforced a hundredfold.

Abraham Lincoln once heard a friend speak angrily of someone. He advised his friend to sit down and write out all of his abuse in a letter. "It will do you good," said Lincoln.

When the letter was written, it was read to Lincoln, who commended it heartily for its severity. The writer was pleased and asked, "When would you advise me to send it?"

"Send it?" replied Lincoln. "Oh, I wouldn't send it. I sometimes write a letter like that. It does me a world of good, but I never send it!"

After writing a memo, review it, and if it's not confidential ask someone else to review it also. Many companies place an almost fanatical emphasis on writing style. A sloppy memo indicates to the reader that your communication was done in haste, without thought, or concern. The recipient feels, "I must not be important enough to this person for her to deeply consider what she is saying to me." Some memos may take you weeks to write and rewrite, making sure there are no misspellings, no ill-chosen words, and no incorrect grammar. Remember, after you drop it in the mail slot, there's no taking it back.

RUMORS

Rumor has it that:

Elvis is alive.
The entire town of Lenox, Mississippi was taken aboard a flying saucer.
Liz Taylor is going to posthumously remarry Richard Burton.

Rumor also has it that:

The Reagans consulted with an astrologer before making decisions.
Imelda Marcos has over 1000 pairs of shoes.
Pete Rose bet on baseball games.
TV wrestling is staged.

Some rumors may have an element of truth, but for the most part it is best to ignore them. When rumors start in an organization that the Japanese are buying out the company, the company is moving to Kalamazoo, or a wage freeze is imminent, it is best to ignore them. Likewise, when rumors start that everyone will get an across-the-board salary increase of 30 percent, a new policy will allow everyone an extra two weeks of vacation, or the company is going to allow flexible hours, it is best to ignore them. By believing in rumors, whether positive or negative, you are doing yourself an emotional disservice.

The allure of a rumor is undeniable. People love to talk about what other people are doing, even if they aren't doing much. Science may never develop a better office intercom than the coffee break. Some people get perverse excitement when telling stories about others. Such stories can lead to career damage, anger, or hurt feelings. If you do hear a juicy rumor that you're dying to spread, think first. What is the possibility that the rumor is false? Don't believe any rumor unless you get it from at least two good sources... who haven't talked to each other. Ask yourself: is the rumor a fair conversational topic; could this rumor cause someone damage? There are times when it is perfectly all right to talk about other people, discuss rumored takeovers and business mergers. Many of us would have little to talk about if we didn't talk about other people. The rule of thumb is: do not spread rumors that could cause damage or hurt in some way, no matter how small.

You could be a walking nervous wreck if you believe in bad rumors. When the rumor subsides, you may feel some relief, but that's like beating your head against a brick wall because it feels so good when you stop. You may overspend on the hope the rumored salary increase will bail you out if you believe in good rumors. When the good rumor doesn't come to fruition you will be in for an emotional and financial downturn. One reason a dog has so many friends is because he wags his tail instead of his tongue.

To demonstrate the futility of rumors, you may try this simple exercise: Write this statement on a piece of paper:

> A red car turned left on a green light and hit a yellow truck on the right back fender. The red car suffered major damage to its left front fender.

Tell one person in a group of six or more people the above message. Ask her to whisper the message down the line of participants. Allow no questions. The last person in line is to tell the group what he heard. You may be surprised at the distortion. This exercise makes one wonder about the accuracy of accident reports and history books.

Rumors may seem too petty a subject to bother with, but unfortunately many careers have been needlessly destroyed by a wily competitor who stooped to using them. In order to stop a rumor you must first know it is being circulated. Avoid spreading rumors yourself but don't cut yourself off from those who spread them. You want to have access to the rumor chain, but you don't want to be perceived as part of the chain. It may be helpful to get an early warning signal, but if your boss or coworkers see you as a rumor spreader, they will be reluctant to trust you with confidential information. To get into the chain you need a loyal subordinate or coworker who will share the news with you without telling others that you were interested and without expecting reciprocal gossip goodies. Be aware, beware, and be prepared. The most damaging kinds of rumors are those that have to do with the way you do your job, or a hint that you are seeking another job or having an intraoffice sexual affair.

As soon as you find out that a rumor has been started about you, confront the originator—in public. Handle the confrontation in a calm, polite manner, never raising your voice or displaying overt anger. An overreaction may convince some people that you're guilty. Like the child caught with his hand in the cookie jar, loudly protesting that he didn't eat the cookies, a loud protest may backfire. If the confrontation is not public, the rumor monger is unlikely to go back and correct the false information.

A well-mannered confrontation might go like this:

BUD: I understand that you have been spreading a rumor that I have been having a relationship with Sue in personnel.

TOM: Gee Bud, I did hear something like that.

BUD: And so you passed it on to a few people.

TOM: I don't know; I may have told a few people.

BUD: Where exactly did you hear this?

TOM: I heard it from a bartender on Bourbon Street.

BUD: I would really like to get to the bottom of this, so suppose you and I go talk to that bartender after work today.

(Bud and Tom have been good friends ever since.)

Remember, that even in the most salacious gossip there is a backhanded compliment being paid to you. People don't gossip about people they deem unimportant, or don't care about at all. Oscar Wilde said it best: "There is only one thing worse than being talked about, and that is not being talked about."

LOOK ME IN THE EYES

It has been said that the eyes are the portals of the soul, and for good reason. Four hundred muscles go into composing the look in your eye and each muscle can create a different look. No other organ of the body communicates as well as the eyes. Making eye contact helps establish trust between people. Too much eye contact (over seven seconds) and the stare can become something else. Lust and love can be communicated as well as hate and mistrust through prolonged eye contact. For business, occasional eye contact for about a second is ideal. When shaking someone's hand, proposing marriage, negotiating a deal, or making a threat, always make direct eye contact. When you are in a situation where it may seem as if you are threatening someone, but you really aren't, pointing your eyes downward often makes you look like less of a threat.

Eye contact is a misnomer in that we can really only look

at one eye at a time. Most people look at the mouth while a person is talking, with only an occasional glance at the eye. Failure to make eye contact will make you appear as if you're not interested or daydreaming.

There is a great children's game that can increase your ability to make eye contact. Simply choose a partner and stare into each other's eyes. The first person to break eye contact is the loser of that round, with a ten-round game. Do not start playing this game without your partner's awareness. Otherwise you may find yourself the catalyst of unwanted lust or even worse, a fist fight.

HEAR YE! HEAR YE! HEAR YE!

> *The most important thing in communication is to hear what isn't being said.*
> —PETER F. DRUCKER

Studies have shown that some 70 to 80 percent of our waking lives is spent communicating, about 45 percent of that time is spent listening, 30 percent in speaking, 16 percent in reading, and 9 percent in writing. (This statistic excludes the loquacious, the taciturn, and the illiterate.) Listening is the most important tool in your tool box . . . at work and in your private relationships.

Listening seems like such a basic skill, we rarely question our ability to do it. Poor listening habits such as daydreaming, doodling, and allowing yourself to be distracted can cause major problems. Yet with practice, anyone can learn to listen well. Why is it that so many people don't bother to pay attention? Probably the chief reason is they don't know they are not listening well. We assume that because a person has two ears attached to his head he knows how to listen. The person you are talking to may hear your words, but a screen of inattention over his mind may block out their meaning. He leaves the discussion with garbled impressions. Yet if you asked him if he had listened, he would be annoyed. "Of course I did!" he would assure you.

When your boss is speaking, demonstrate your ability to listen, and don't expect the boss to pay you the same courtesy. Some people think the best way to get a promotion is to dazzle the boss with intellect and ability. The fact is, the boss does not like a subordinate that appears more intelligent or more capable than he is. Studies have shown that the way to get someone to like you is to show interest in what he is saying and to demonstrate that you like him. When the boss tells a story of yesteryear, show interest and refer to the story in subsequent conversations. The boss's idea of intelligence is someone who listens to him.

There are four basic causes of poor listening habits:

1. We don't realize that listening is a skill that must be learned like any other, and sharpened by constant practice.
2. We don't recognize the value of listening because we are so busy trying to express our own ideas.
3. We don't like to listen because we aren't interested; besides, we have to listen to too much anyway.
4. We don't know how to go about improving our listening habits, even if we admit they are far from perfect.

The following are a few suggestions for developing better listening habits.

Put thought speed to work to improve your listening habits. It is estimated that the speed of thought moves four to five times faster that the speed of speech. All of this time allows your mind to wander, daydream, or focus on one point with which you disagree and plan to knock down as soon as you have the opportunity. As a result, you aren't fully informed on the speaker's ideas; this may destroy the effectiveness of your rebuttal.

This doesn't mean that the only time to listen is when you disagree. It does suggest that you can profit by the advantage that the speed of thought has over the speed of speech to improve your listening skills.

Read the thoughts behind the words. The tones of the speaker's voice, facial expression and body language are revealing clues to his real opinions. The way the speaker emphasizes a particular point may reveal his biases, preferences, and where his knowledge may be either lacking or not quite adequate. By keeping your eyes on the speaker, you will stay alert and attentive.

Summarize. Another way to use the lag between speech and thought is to summarize frequently what the speaker has said. The fact that your mind is working on what the speaker says improves your listening skill. One of the greatest faults in listening is to sit with fake attention while your mind has wandered somewhere else.

Use questions. It is difficult to keep your mind at the peak of concentration for long periods of time. When you lose the trend of the speaker's discourse, a question will snap you back to full attention. "Would you mind explaining that last point a little more fully?" is the sort of question that puts patches on a listening blowout.

Understand the intended meaning of the speaker's words. The same words mean different things to different people. If you don't understand the speaker's use of a word or phrase, ask her to define it. A misunderstood word or phrase can start you in the wrong direction and cause you to come to a totally false conclusion.

Keep an open mind. If you don't like the speaker or have little respect for his ideas, you should still try to be objective. Don't let your prejudices interfere with your ability to listen. Everyone is entitled to have his or her say, and it's your job to listen. Communications work only when there's a two-way flow.

Do not make a rebuttal too quickly. Hear the speaker out before you make a counter argument. If you break in to correct the speaker's mistakes, the issue in dispute may never be clearly defined. Try to follow the speaker's discourse by looking at the issue from his side. You may even go so far as to think up supporting arguments he may have overlooked that would strengthen his position. Having a thorough understanding of the opposing point of view will enable you to prepare a better rebuttal.

Stay focused on the main idea. The good listener isn't sidetracked by extraneous or inconsequential remarks that screen main thoughts. Once the good listener has a firm grasp of the basic point the speaker is making, everything else falls into place.

There are four levels of listening. At level one we hear physically, but there is no processing of what we hear. An example is the hum of your computer or air conditioner.

At level two, we hear but we don't listen. The sad fact is that it is at this level many of us sink when listening to our "significant other." This can create major problems in a relationship.

A man came home from work and his wife greeted him at the door with a cold beer and the evening newspaper. She gave him a big kiss and ushered him to his recliner. She took off his shoes, massaged his feet, and curled up in a chair next to him. Just as he was getting to the sports section his wife said, "Honey, would you take out the garbage tonight?" He said, "Oh, sure, Honey." She said, "And would you take the dog for a walk?" Now deeply into the sports section he replied, "Oh, sure, Honey." "And by the way, I had an affair with the mailman today." Nearing the bottom of his beer he said, "Oh, sure, Honey."

At level three we hear words and understand them. At times

we can even repeat them verbatim. To hear words and *understand what is really meant* one must progress to level four.

At level four, the listener looks at the speaker's body language, makes eye contact, and observes facial expressions. Nonverbals carry 55 percent of the actual meaning of our statements. To really understand what someone is saying you must look at her while she speaks.

When the boss rushes into your office, taps on your desk, makes direct eye contact, and says, "Can you get this out in an hour?" She is not asking a question.

Karl Menninger said, "Listening is a magnetic and strange thing, a creative force. The friends who listen to us are the ones we move toward, and we want to sit in their radius. When we are listened to, it creates us, makes us unfold and expand."

SMALL TALK

Small talk is unimportant conversation. It's chit-chat between two or more friends about an up-coming football game, an apple pie recipe, or how well they ran in Saturday's 10k. Knowing how to make small talk is a useful tool. It can be used to fill embarrassing silent moments in a conversation, relax, and if you are really good at it, entertain. Small talk can be used to charm or flatter someone and to show off a sense of humor. The very essence of nightclub chatter is small talk.

When you're ill at ease, small talk becomes difficult. When you're accidentally seated next to the CEO of your company, first meeting the potential love of your life, or seated around a conference table waiting for a meeting to start, small talk becomes difficult. Nervous tension builds up, you feel droplets of sweat forming under your arm pits and you're tongue-tied. In these situations it is often hard to think of something to say. Having a group of topics to choose from already in mind can help: topics such as sports, the antics of the Royal Family, movies, books, favorite restaurants, clothes, and if all else fails, the weather. A few topics to avoid are the wart on your little finger, your sex life, dirty jokes, and harmful gossip.

One of the biggest taboos of small talk is to ask a coworker how much money he or she makes, and it's even worse manners to tell how much you make. Income varies so much among personnel of equal position that disclosure of income may cause anger and disappointment. In some companies, the disclosure of income is cause for dismissal. In a survey of five hundred executives, 85 percent said they would rather disclose the intimate details of their sex lives than disclose their incomes. William Shakespeare said, "Conversation should be pleasant without scurrility, witty without affectation, free without indecency, learned without conceitedness, novel without falsehood."

HUMOR HELPS

Wit is the salt of conversation, not the food.
—WILLIAM HAZLITT

A sense of humor is the pole that adds balance to our steps as we walk the tightrope of life. Humor can be the deciding factor in many difficult situations. The more serious the subject or situation, the more valuable humor can be in easing tensions. When you make a mistake, laugh at yourself; people will laugh with you rather than at you. Laughter is like a diaper change. Not a permanent solution, just something that makes life tolerable.

A group of 284 high school students was asked to rate their teachers according to teaching ability and also the use of humor in the classroom. In every case the teacher that ranked high in teaching ability also ranked high in use of humor. Executives often assume the role of teacher via their example of their authoritative position. A sense of humor can make a valuable contribution to the effectiveness of a leader or to any other position in life.

Not only is humor good for your leadership effectiveness, it's also good for your health. Norman Cousins' experiences with the healing powers of humor vividly demonstrate the awesome power of humor. Cousins was suffering from a degenerative spinal condition brought on by a type of endocrine imbalance that can be caused by tension and anxiety. His doctors gave him 500 to 1 odds against recovery. Cousins wondered if positive feelings could undo what negative feelings had wrought. He moved from his hospital room to a hotel room and barricaded himself with humor. He rented Marx Brothers movies, Candid Camera tapes, and other humorous films. Within a few years he was completely cured. If humor can cure a monstrous disease, don't you think it could help you cope with a few mosquitoes?

The two best uses of executive humor are to defuse tense situations and to create rapport. Eugene Cafiero, then president of Chrysler, went to England to meet with workers at a troubled plant. When he was ushered in to meet the angry unionists, a man ran up to him and yelled in his face, "I'm Nick Mikowsky and I'm a Communist." The witty executive said "How do you do. I'm Eugene Cafiero and I'm a Presbyterian." The roar of laughter cleared the air so they could get down to business. Laughter is the most potent, constructive force for diffusing business tension in the known universe. If you can point out what is humorous or absurd about a situation or confrontation, the tension will melt like butter. In business jargon this is known as "greasing the skids." Psychologists say that we have only four basic emotions: glad, sad, mad, and scared. Humor can move us from sad, mad, or scared to glad, which is the state all of us prefer.

Some executives are skilled at using humor to build rapport with their subordinates. A self-deprecating jest with a subordinate can for a moment eclipse the differences in their relative status and create a chance for real communication. Sarcastic witticisms at the expense of others serve to reduce rapport and heighten status differences.

Humor, if used inappropriately, can be deadly. Sometimes a man who thinks of himself as a wit may be only half right. Unless you are the CEO, in which case everyone has to laugh at your jokes, it is inappropriate to open a presentation at a business meeting with an anecdote or joke. Likewise, don't make wisecracks during a meeting or with your superiors, unless you know them well and can predict how your comments will be perceived. Once labeled as a joker, you may be overlooked for more serious assignments. A skillful use of humor at the right time can diffuse a tense situation or vividly illustrate a point. Using humor can make people laugh at you or with you, depending on your ability to use it.

CROSS-CULTURAL BLOOPERS

The phone rang; the voice on the other end said, "I understand you teach a conflict resolution seminar; we need you in Jakarta right away. We have some Indonesians on the warpath. Yesterday they chased one of our foremen around with a fire axe. The Superintendent intervened just in time. I don't know what's going on. Get on over here and see what you can do."

The next day our hero boarded a 727 and twenty-five hours later deplaned in a culture vastly different from his own. The long plane ride gave him time for a crash course in Indonesian culture. With ample knowledge of Louisiana Red Neck behavior, he felt sure he knew the source of the problem.

The solution was to educate the American expatriates on proper Indonesian etiquette: never touch an Indonesian on the head, this is the location of the soul; never touch an Indonesian with your left hand, the left hand is considered unclean; never point at Indonesians or show them the soles of your feet, this is considered offensive; and never stand with your arms akimbo, this is considered aggressive.

The poor foreman had committed all of these bloopers. He was sitting down with his feet propped up (exposing the souls of his feet). He pointed to one of his workers and told him to "Come over here!" The foreman stood up with his arms akimbo, and said, "Go get me a cup of coffee." The worker went to get the foreman a cup of coffee, mixing in just the right amount of cream and sugar, the way the foreman likes it. He brought the coffee, the foreman took a sip, got up and patted the worker on the head with his left hand and said, "You do good work, boy." All of these cultural bloopers were too much for the Indonesian; he grabbed a fire axe, screamed, and chased the foreman around the desk. The Superintendent intervened just in time to save the foreman's head.

After a few classes in cross-cultural norms and expectations, of both Indonesians and Americans, the situation greatly improved.

TELEPHONE TACTICS

> *I don't mind being placed on "hold" but sometimes I think they've got me on "ignore."*
> —AUTHOR UNKNOWN

In the United States about 55 percent of all business is done over the telephone. The way you present yourself on the phone is a reflection of you and your company. When you talk on the telephone the listener cannot see your face; therefore the accuracy of your message must be communicated through your tone of voice and the words you use. If you have a weak voice, you must work on making it sound stronger and if you have a flat, monotone voice you'll want to work on making it sound more lively.

Answer the phone by saying your first and last name. Use a tone that indicates you are pleased someone has called and you are eager to help them. Go up an octave on the last syllable of the last name.

Being gruff or abrupt when answering the phone can put callers on the defensive. A conflict situation is created at the onset of the conversation.

Devote all of your attention to the caller. Don't shuffle papers, chew gum, or tuck the phone under your chin. Speak directly into the transmitter and articulate clearly.

If the caller asks for someone in your department or for someone you don't know, try to be helpful. Don't say, "You've got the wrong department," followed by a click as you hang up. Make an effort to help the caller locate the person.

If you reach a wrong number when calling someone, do not hang up. Instead say, "Is this 484–7952?" The party you reached will say, "No," and you can then apologize and hang up quickly.

It is best to make and take your own calls. It adds a personal touch. If you feel your time is far too valuable to waste on such maundane chores, then you may insist that a secretary do this. If a secretary places your calls, do not waste people's time by having the call placed and then keeping the person you had called waiting.

The secretary represents you when making calls for you. It is important to make sure that this person handles your calls the way you want them handled. Instruct the secretary about whether or not you want to know who is calling before you answer the phone. This information is best obtained by asking, "May I ask who is calling, please?" This is a very touchy question and must be handled with great tact and diplomacy. If your secretary asks this question and you are unable to accept the call, the caller may get the impression you don't want to talk to her.

Never ask your secretary to lie for you. If you can't come to the phone, your secretary can say you are *not available*, rather than saying you're out of the office when you aren't.

> SECRETARY: Your wife wants to give you a kiss over the phone.
> BOSS: Take a message and give it to me later.

Many companies today are encouraging executives to place their own calls. This is more considerate of others and saves time—especially the secretaries'.

Before making a call, jot down what you want to talk about and the results you hope to achieve. Focus your conversation on these topics.

When placing a call, identify yourself immediately, saying "This is Donald Trump of Trump Enterprises. May I speak to Mr. Lee Ioccoca, please?" Don't say, "Let me speak to Lee," or "Is Lee there?" The person answering the phone should not have to ask who is calling.

Once connected, get to the point of the call first, then engage in small talk as time may allow. Most people call and say, "Hey Charlie, how's the weather up there, did you play some golf over the weekend," etc. This small talk may go on for five minutes or more before getting to the point of the phone call. When you are called and the caller wishes to engage in small talk first, you have little choice but to listen. When you call someone, get to the point and engage in small talk later, otherwise you're wasting the time of the person you called.

In social calls it is polite to have the caller who initiated the call also indicate when the call is over. In business your time is too important to allow for this formality. If your time is being wasted, sign off gracefully, even if you did not initiate the call.

To get rid of a long-winded caller you may say, "I really don't want to waste any more of your time, so I'll say good-bye now."

End phone calls by saying "Good-bye." Don't say "Bye-bye," or as one Texas executive was fond of saying, "Ten-four on your mashed potatoes." A good-bye may not be necessary if it is clear to both parties that the phone call is over.

How many of us have gone through the following dialogue when trying to reach someone:

    8:00 A.M.: "He hasn't come in yet."
    9:00 A.M.: "I expect him any minute."
  10:00 A.M.: "He just called and said he'd be late."
  11:00 A.M.: "He just came in, but he stepped away from his desk."
  11:45 A.M.: "He's gone to lunch."
    1:00 P.M.: "I expect him back any minute."
    1:30 P.M.: "He hasn't come back yet. Can I take a message?"
    2:30 P.M.: "He's somewhere in the building. His coat is here."
    3:30 P.M.: "He went out again. I don't know when he'll be back."
    4:30 P.M.: "No, he's gone for the day."

Telephone tag can be avoided. When you can't reach the other party the first time you call, don't leave your number for her to call back. Instead, ask when she will be available, then say you will call back then. Another tactic is to establish a very narrow time frame for calling back: "Please tell President Bush that I will try to reach reach him this afternoon between 1:30 and 1:45 P.M." He will schedule commitments around your call.

ANSWERING MACHINES AND SERVICES

Some people hate answering machines. It seems unreasonable for these people to bear animosity toward this useful device. It is rude not to leave a message when your call is answered by a machine. The person receiving the aborted message must listen to thirty minutes of dial tone and wonder who called. Always leave a message; if your call is unimportant, leave the message that your call is unimportant and a return call is not necessary. Always leave your name, number, what company you are from, the date and time, and say whether or not you want a return call.

Answering services sometimes sound as if you have actually reached the secretary of the party you are calling. You may ask for information that the answering service does not know. The people who work for answering services are hired to take messages and pass them on. They have many different clients and have no information about any of them. Pumping them for information will do you no good and is rude. Simply leave your message and don't ask unreasonable questions.

DON'T SAY DON'T

It is well to remember that grammar is common speech formulated.

—W. SOMERSET MAUGHAM

Knowing how to use words correctly is the mark of an educated person. It is also the mark of a promotable person. The proper use of the English language is learnable. Many learn it; during childhood if they had parents that corrected every word; others must play catch-up. The following list consists of frequently misused words and grammatical errors:

DON'T—Don't say *don't* when you should say *doesn't*. A simple way to know when to say one or the other is to do away with the contraction. The sentence will then sound awkward. An example is: "She don't love me anymore." With the contraction left out it reads, "She do not love me anymore." This sounds fine if you are playing a native in an old Tarzan movie. More palatable is: "She doesn't love me anymore." Without the contraction it reads, "She does not love me anymore."

BETWEEN versus AMONG—*Between* refers to an exchange involving two persons: if there are three or more people, use *among*. (Incorrect: Clare, among you and I, I think the whole thing stinks.)

BETWEEN YOU AND I—The correct expression is *between you and me*. (See the above example.)

CAN and MAY—*Can* means the ability to do something. *May* means permission to do it. (Incorrect: Can I take you to the prom?)

DIALOGUE—Help fight fancy English. Why use *dialogue* when the word *talk* will do just as well? (You low down dirt-bag; I think it's time we had a dialogue.)

END RESULT—A result is the end. Use one or the other. (Incorrect: The final end result was inconclusive.)

FARTHER versus FURTHER—*Farther* should be reserved for conveying ideas of physical distance. Use *further* for everything else. The distinction between these two words will probably disappear eventually; as Theodore Berstein points out in *The Careful Writer*, "It looks as if farther is going to be mowed down by the scythe of Old Further Time."

GIVE ME, GET ME, LET ME—Be sure to pronounce these as two separate words. ("Gimme the ball and lemmie show my stuff.")

HOUSE versus HOME—A *house* is a building and a *home*

is a spiritual dwelling place. (Incorrect: House, sweet house.)

IRREGARDLESS—There is no such word! *Irregardless* is a redundancy. Use *regardless*. I didn't learn this until my forty-third birthday.

JOKE versus ANECDOTE—A *joke* is something said or done to provoke laughter while an *anecdote* is a short narrative of an interesting, amusing, or biographical incident. Comedians tell jokes; humorists tell anecdotes.

KUDOS—This always takes a singular verb. There is no such thing as a *kudo*.

LAY versus LIE—*Lay* means to place or put down. *Lie* means to recline. Chickens lay eggs, people lie down.

NEITHER versus EITHER—*Neither* always goes with *nor* and *either* always goes with *or*. With both words either the "e" or "i" pronunciations are fine.

OFF—Never use this in place of *from*. I got a big kiss off Harriett," is illiterate.

PEOPLE versus PERSONS—Use *people* for large groups and *persons* for an exact or small number. ("The American people lament the fate of the eight persons being held as hostages.")

QUEUE versus CUE—*Queue* means to line up or wait in a queue and *cue* is a signal to an actor to begin a specific speech. In China a queue is a braid of hair worn hanging from the back of the head. In a pool hall a cue is a ball used to strike other balls. Never go into a Chinese pool hall and ask for the cue ball . . . you may be given a ball of hair.

RESTROOM versus BATHROOM—A *restroom* is used to refer to public facilities while a *bathroom* is found in the home.

SHALL versus WILL—The old grammatical distinction is

a thing of the past. Don't worry about the rules, just let your ear be your guide. "We shall overcome" is just as correct as "We will overcome."

TOMATO and AUNT—The broad "a" is just as correct as the short "a" in *aunt* or the long "a" in *tomato*. Say whatever feels comfortable to you.

WHICH and WHO—Use *who* when referring to a person and *which* when referring to things.

YOU KNOW—This has filtered into our language since the early 1960s and it irritates the older group to no end. To them, it's a sign of rebellion and lazy thinking. Other youthful expressions to avoid are: oh, man; hey, cool; really, like (as in, "hey that's really, like, cool, man"); oh, wow; you know; mellow-out; go for it; far out; groovy; that's hip; what a guy; have a nice day; share with you; relate to you; check it out; and class act.

Never greet an executive by asking, "Hey, dude, what's happening?" The chances are he doesn't know what's happening and if he did it would be confidential information anyway.

Each section of the country has its own vernacular. Using local dialect may be acceptable when you are talking to one of your own. If you go outside of your region you may not be understood, as when a Texas gal was dining in an Ohio restaurant. In response to the hostess's offer to get her anything she needed, the Yellow Rose said, "Ah could use some rotten pepper." The perplexed hostess inquired: "What's that?" The Lone Star Lady explained: "You know, Honey, rotten pepper, so ah can rot a letter home."

Foul language and business mixes about as well as oil and water, particularly in mixed company. No matter how many times we hear the four-letter "F" word in movies, the senses are still shocked when someone cusses in the middle of a business chat. There is nothing pleasant about hearing supposedly intelligent people use scatological language. Vulgar language is gross and uncalled-for in business conversations. Some words are more offensive than others. An occasional "damn" or "hell," may be effectively used for emphasis, without offending most people's sensibilities.

Cursing at inanimate objects when no one else is present is a great release. As Mark Twain said, "Under certain circumstances, profanity provides a relief denied even in prayer."

In some occupations a little profanity is actually expected: A rancher in Texas had to confront the new federal statute prohibiting job classification by sex. He finally ran the following ad in the local newspaper: "Cowperson wanted. Applicant must use profanity and share a bunkhouse with five male cowpersons who seldom bathe."

One must also avoid misplaced modifiers. A misplaced modifier gives the false impression that it modifies a word or group of words, but what it actually modifies has been left out of the sentence. For example:

> "Being old and dog-eared, I was able to buy the book for 50 cents."
> "Walking along the shore, a fish suddenly jumped out of the water."
> "When dipped in butter, you can taste the lobster's delicious flavor."

Malapropisms, mixed metaphors and scrambled language are found in newspapers across the country:

> "This has all the earmarks of an eyesore."
> "I deny allegation and defy the alligator."
> "Let's grab the bull by the tail and look the facts squarely in the face."
> "The roosters have come home to hatch."
> "You can't straddle the fence and still keep your ear to the ground."

Some other common yet subtle vulgarizations of language include:

"Hi," instead of "Hello"
"Sure" instead of "Of course"
"Yeah" instead of "Yes"
"Sure" instead of "Surely"
"Wait a sec" instead of "Will you please wait?"
"Goin'" instead of "Going"
"Comin'" instead of "Coming"
"Com'ere" instead of "Come here"
"Ain't" instead of "Isn't"
"De" instead of "The"

These stiff-sounding expressions sound good to a stranger. They add formality and elegance to the image of the speaker and indicate that you are willing to make the extra effort to observe the formalities of respect when addressing clients and business associates.

The way we speak was taught to us from early childhood. Changing our vernacular takes constant vigilance and practice, but then you may decide never to leave Lubbock.

TONE OF VOICE

It's not enough just to use the right words, you must also use the right tone and timing. A person with a high nasal voice that speaks rapidly carries little authority. Remember Barney Fife's voice on "The Andy Grifith Show?" He got no respect. If you are one of these people you should practice lowering the tone of your voice an octave and speaking more slowly. Remember, 38 percent of the meaning of your message is communicated through your tone of voice.

A well-known technique for maintaining discipline in the

classroom is not to yell at the child. Yelling shows that your leadership is teetering. Lowering your voice and slowly saying, "Jerome, if you don't stop playing with that, I'm going to take it away from you," is much more effective than a high-pitched, hysterical voice.

Clint Eastwood would not be effective in his threat if he had rapidly said in a high voice, "Go ahead, make my day."

The sentence, "I didn't say he stole the money," can give five different messages, depending on how you emphasize just one word. If I say "*I* didn't say he stole the money," the sentence means, "Don't accuse me of saying he stole the money." If I say, "I didn't *say* he stole the money," this sentence means, "I didn't say he stole the money, I only implied it." If I say, "I didn't say he *stole* the money," perhaps he just borrowed it instead. And if I say, "I didn't say he stole the *money*," perhaps he stole the jewels instead.

Careful attention to the tone of your voice—the pitch, timing, and emphasis—can make you a better communicator.

CHAPTER NINE

PERSONALITY

THE PURPOSE OF this chapter is not to introduce therapeutic techniques designed to correct major personality problems. It does contain behavioral mosquitoes that may interfere with your success at the office and suggest some ways of dealing with them.

LIKABILITY

> *A loving person lives in a loving world. A hostile person lives in a hostile world: everyone you meet is your mirror.*
>
> —KEN KEYES, JR.

Likability is vastly underrated as an element in corporate success. Journalists love to write articles about CEOs who are mean, vile, and unscrupulous. On television, businessmen are always the heavy. J.R. on "Dallas" has become the stereotypical wheeler-dealer. As a result, many people forget that

142

likability is a desirable trait in business. Being able to get along with others is an asset, not a liability. I'm not talking about being soft or easily manipulated. What I am talking about is a personality that others like to work for/with in an atmosphere of mutual respect. If two candidates are considered for the same position, and both are equally qualified, the most likable candidate will get the job. If the likable candidate is less qualified, she is still likely to get the job.

Some people get fired simply because they are disliked, either by a boss or even the people who work for Mr. Nasty. It's hard to motivate a group of people when they hate your guts. If you're likable, you don't even have to be good at your job; you can coast on mediocre performance for quite a while.

C. Wright Mills said, "When white-collar people get jobs, they sell not only their time and energy, but their personalities as well. They sell by week, or month, their smiles and kindly gestures, and they must practice prompt repression of resentment and aggression."

THE COMPANY SHRINK

> *Confession may be good for the soul but it is bad for the reputation.*
>
> —THOMAS DEWAR

Don't spill your guts to the company shrink. Most company shrinks are not company employees. They are usually outside psychologists whose main purpose is to share the blame with upper management for personnel decisions.

You may think you're having a confidential chat but that is far from reality. The shrink must file a report of your visit and a notation of the report is placed in your personnel file. Upper management has access to the full report when making personnel decisions. If the report indicates that you are discontented with management or your job, you may not get the promotion.

Company shrinks also do "in-depth interviews" to help management make personnel decisions. Again, this is not the forum to "ventilate your feelings." Interviewees should never reveal the skeletons in their closets. When taking this type of interview, it helps to visualize yourself as a boy or girl scout. Say nothing negative, yet show you are assertive. It's a balancing act, so be careful, it's easy to fall.

During this interview, you may be subjected to a number of tests, none of which have much validity. Intelligence tests, developed by Alfred Bienet in 1905, were first used to cull retarded children from the general population. Today there are many forms of this original test, designed to cull out retarded executives. Three of the most popular are the Wechsler Adult Intelligence Scale, the very difficult Miller Analogies Test and the Wonderlick. The first two are more involved than the Wonderlick. The Wonderlick only takes twelve minutes to administer and there is no law preventing anyone from using it. The other two require a licensed shrink. Most still use the Wonderlick because it takes less time and it is easy to administer. Your entire career may hang on how well you perform during those twelve minutes.

Some argue that a major problem with intelligence tests is that they may be culturally biased. The tests do not take cultural differences into account. If you spent most of your life in Harlem, in a different country, or in an extremely rural area of the United States, the test might be more difficult for you even though your IQ is quite normal or even above normal. Nevertheless, management will weigh the results of this test above interpersonal skills and technical expertise. Busy managers may not want to wade through all of the report and simply jump to the part about IQ. If you are not above normal, you will likely be eliminated. Since these tests are timed, the trick is to go through the test as quickly as possible answering the questions you know, and then go back and ponder over the ones you don't know. If you know you are going to take an IQ test, try to find out which one will be administered. It may be worth your time and money to contact a psychologist and ask her to give you the test. You may or may not get the exact test, but you will be more familiar with the format and types of questions.

In 1988, the Office of Technology Assessment banned the use of polygraph tests from most private-sector organizations. This test can still be used for government jobs and for a few private-sector jobs. These tests are not considered reliable.

Personality-based tests try to determine if you might be inclined to deviant behavior, including theft at the workplace. Many of the questions set you up so you must lie, because to tell the truth would make you fail the test. Professor Dershowitz of Harvard says, "Truly honest people, who reveal proclivities, have to fail the test. I think the people who deserve a ticket to heaven are those who do have proclivities and overcome them."

All the major publishers produce studies to prove that the tests are valid. "True," says Nancy Carson, director of the OTA study, "but most of their evidence comes from studies which might not be considered as being at arm's length. We have not concluded our analysis."

Representative Williams, awaiting the OTA study, says: "These tests bring to mind that song about the frontier judge who wanted to make sure the guilty wouldn't get away: He sentenced everybody to hang."

ASSESSMENT CENTERS

Because company shrinks and psychological tests are not that wonderful as predictors of managerial success, many companies have turned to the assessment center. AT&T pioneered the use of assessment centers in the late 1950s. Today they have spread to include most of the Fortune 500.

Assessment centers usually consist of six to eight members that are one or two rungs above you. Included on the committee is at least one person from personnel that will be the gofer and all-around administrative assistant for the group. The company shrink may also be included. Typically, you will first have to make a ten-to-twelve minute presentation on the question, "Tell us about yourself." You will be expected to stand before this esteemed group and confidently tell them a digested version of your life history. The committee hears all of the candidates first and then breaks into pairs for individual interviewing. The candidate will be interviewed by all of the subcommittees, sometimes having four or five interviews in one day. After this, the candidates are dismissed and the committee meets to compare notes and make assessments of all the individuals. A week or so later the candidates will be notified as to their acceptance or rejection for a given position. Some companies use this as a means of identifying their fast-track people for future promotions.

Other companies use different structures for their assessment centers, the most common being the use of the "in-basket." The candidate is told it is Sunday morning at the office—no one is around for you to call or consult. You are given three hours to go through a heaping in-basket test. You must decide what to do with a host of managerial problems you will encounter in the in-basket. The trick is to go through the entire basket first and group related items into piles.

Some assessment centers use team exercise for financial cases, to determine leadership capabilities and interpersonal skills. Talking a lot seems to increase leadership scores. William Byham of Development Dimensions International, which helps companies design assessment centers, said, "Timing is so important. On the leaderless group discussion, somebody will have been told that the thing to do is to call for a vote.

He'll call for a vote four times, and be promptly voted down each time."

Assessment centers are costly; usually the meeting is conducted at an off-plant site to eliminate phone calls and other interruptions. This means lunch is provided for everyone. The managerial time consumed assessing and the travel expenses of all involved can run up the tab very quickly.

The best thing about assessment centers is that they are designed for a specific company, and use company managers as assessors. The illegal question, "Is he one of us?" will be answered without actually being asked. This gives the assessment center one up on the sending-someone-out-to-be-tested approach.

YOUR BOSS IS NOT YOUR MOTHER

Treat your boss in the same manner that you treat the company shrink. Don't use your boss as a therapist: he or she is not a person who wants to hear your personal problems. If you must have a shoulder to cry on, choose a close personal friend, spouse, or private therapist. It's also best to save your co-workers from the bleeding heart. You may need to inform your boss about some problem, a health problem or death in the family, but always let him or her know that you have the situation under control and it won't affect your job for long. Talking about your problems to you boss will get you labeled as a whiner, an excuse maker. Bosses like the strong, silent type that brings in the ship without firing distress flares.

THE ASSERTIVE WIMP

Many companies sponsor "Assertiveness Training Seminars." Their intention is not to make the employee more assertive.

Companies do not want employees saying "No" without guilt when they are given an assignment they prefer not to do.

Companies do want their salesmen to have enough assertiveness to make cold calls, to uphold company policy, and be able to negotiate on behalf of the company. It's a balancing act between being assertive and being a wimp. Samuel Goldwyn once said, "I don't want any yes-men around me. I want someone to tell the truth—even if it costs him his job."

Dr. Alex Horrniman of the University of Virginia's Darden School defines assertiveness through the following story:

Do you remember the Saturday night sock hops in high school? There were five types of people that attended those dances:

Ones drove to the dance but never got out of their car, in fact many ended up hiding in their trunk.

Twos drove to the dance, got out of their cars, but never made it into the dance. They stayed outside saying things like, "It costs too much. I don't like to dance. The band is awful, etc."

Threes drove to the dance, got out of their cars, went into the dance, and became wallflowers. They sat around hoping someone would ask them to dance, but no one ever did.

Fours drove to the dance, went into the dance, and danced the night away.

Fives drove to the dance, went into the dance, and danced until they found someone special, and then brought them back to their cars.

The ultimate drag in life is to be a One trapped in the trunk of a Five's car. Essentially, companies are asking their employees to be Fours, because Fives are too aggressive, are likely to start their own business, and often get into sexual harassment litigation.

IT'S NICE TO BE IMPORTANT BUT IT'S MORE IMPORTANT TO BE NICE

When we get really busy, it's easy to forget to be nice to people. No matter how pressured you feel, take the time to smile and say hello to fellow employees. In the self-centered world of the "Me Generation," courtesy, politeness, and respect for the rights of others are often subordinated to self-interest.

Some believe that acting nice indicates weakness, irresolution, or a "soft touch," but take a close look at some adjectives that describe the opposite of nice: mean-spirited; callous; insensitive; unconcerned; and malevolent. These are not desirable characteristics.

The "nice" manager is rewarded by employees who are loyal and hard-working. The reverse is also true.

A manager returned from a Management Development Program and said to his secretary, "Sue, I've learned from my seminar that I've been doing everything wrong. I'm no longer going to make you type my personal letters, pick up my dry cleaning or call you a bimbo." Sue said, "OK, boss, let me get this straight, you're no longer going to make me type your personal letters, pick up your dry cleaning or call me a bimbo, is that right?" The Executive said, "That's right." Sue said, "In that case, boss, I will no longer spit in your coffee."

The moral is, When you're nasty to your employees, you never know when they are spitting in your coffee.

GIVE IT TO THEM THE WAY THEY WANT IT

When you come up with a great new business idea, you should propose it to your boss before mentioning it to anyone else.

Let your boss present the idea to his boss. He may or may not give you credit: that should not be your major concern. Your boss knows it was your idea and will remember that when raise/promotion time rolls around. If he forgets, give him a gentle reminder.

When you go to your boss with your great idea, make sure it is well thought out and realistic. Design your presentation in a way that he will be most receptive. There is no one correct way to make a presentation.

Different folks require different strokes. Some managers will require great detail, research, multiple bids and more and more information before making a decision. For this manager your monthly activities report should be thick, filled with details, statistics, and anything else that indicates intelligence.

Other managers require the personal touch. Monthly reports may be delivered orally in a monthly meeting. Written or oral, the report should mention community activities, problem personalities, staff parties, and anything else that reflects that you are a warm, feeling person.

Still other managers feel they are much too busy to deal with detail or personal feelings. They want the facts. Make your report short, to the point, and with no fillers. Your one-page report should reflect the bare bones of what you're doing. Do not speak of problems you are having, speak only of results.

If you want to sell yourself, your idea, or your product, you must give managers information in the way they like it. Selling is a little like hog calling—it isn't the noise you make, it's the appeal in your voice.

A JOB IS NOT A HOME

Don't be lulled by your job into a feeling of security. There are no secure jobs in America today. The federal government is scaling back, in the military it's either "up or out," tenure means little in the school system today, and all companies have ups and downs. No company hands out certificates for guaranteed lifetime employment. Do not become complacent; always strive to make yourself more marketable. The watch word today is not so much employment but employability.

Some workaholics forsake their families, hobbies, social events, and all noncompany activities for their jobs. These people have the hardest time adjusting when laid off and die soon after retirement.

THE EIGHT MOST LETHAL MOSQUITOES

The most lethal mosquito of all is if your company doubts your integrity. No employer would have someone working for her that she didn't trust. A study conducted by Burke Marketing Research reported that if a company believes that an employee lacks integrity, all positive qualities—ranging from skill to experience to productivity and intelligence—become meaningless.

Most often, untrustworthy employees will trick themselves up by inflating their expense accounts. They gather fake receipts while on business trips, have their spouse bring them to the airport and report they took a taxi, stay in the best hotels and eat at the best restaurants. Some plan a "business trip" around their prearranged vacations. Most likely the boss has made these business trips before and knows about how much your trip cost. If you're going to lie, cheat and steal from your employer, you'd better be very good at covering yourself because over the long term there are many different ways you can be found out. Before becoming a petty thief, ask yourself, *Is it worth it?* Remember, if you get fired for petty theft, it will haunt you for the rest of your life.

The seven other lethal mosquitoes are listed in decreasing order of seriousness.

Having a conflict of interest. A sideline business that you conduct at the office, such as running a bookie joint or dating service will get you fired every time. This also includes kickbacks from suppliers, profiting from inside information, and any other act wherein you place self-interest before doing the job you were hired to do.

Undependable and irresponsible. If you do not get your work in on time and with the agreed-upon quality, you will gain a reputation as being undependable.

Cockiness, brashness, and a huge ego. Bosses have large egos and they don't want the competition. The only thing that bragging about your accomplishments all the time will get you is the boot out the back door.

Absenteeism and poor punctuality. If you're not there, how can you possibly get the job done?

Not following the boss's orders or circumventing company policy. This includes disobeying dress codes, going over your boss's head and not getting approval for activities before you do them. In business jargon this is called the "End Run."

Being a whiner. People who are always whining and complaining aren't appreciated anywhere. One complainer in an office can cast a pall over fellow workers, destroy morale, and demotivate the motivated.

Being an unconcerned, lazy slob. Executives work an average of fifty-six hours a week, and they certainly do not work any less on the way up. In the corporate world, work is no harder at the top than it is in middle management. Most executives will say hard work is the reason for their success, not politics, image, or manners. They may be right to some degree, but having the right political connections, a polished image and good manners certainly played a part in their ascent.

An article in Parade magazine entitled "Why They Excel" explained why Asian-American students are winning top honors in school and getting the best jobs when they graduate. Essentially, the Asian-Americans work harder. Hispanics do an average of 3.98 hours of homework a week, blacks 4.23 hours, non-Hispanic whites 6.12 hours, and Asian-Americans do an average of 7.03. A survey of 7000 students in San Francisco–area high schools found that Asian-American–consistently get better grades than any other group of students, regardless of their parents' level of education or their families' socioeconomic status, the usual predictors of success. No difference in IQ was found; the only difference was hard work.

For executives to average fifty-six hours per week they have to make sacrifices. They have to be willing to take calls on weekends, to work at home—even on Sundays—and spend less time with their families. Executives who work these brutal hours often report that they actually enjoy working. They get the same satisfaction from working that other people get from hobbies or sports. They aren't really working; they are playing in the sandbox.

CHAPTER TEN

HOW TO GET CONTROL OF THE LITTLE THINGS

Men often bear little grievances with less courage than they do large misfortunes.

—AESOP

THE "LITTLE THINGS" in life can not only stifle your career, but can also make you ill. Recent studies indicate that the ordinary little irritations of life can give rise to a wide variety of mental and physical problems. Long before there was research on little things, Ben Franklin said, "Little strokes fell great oaks."

Most of us can easily handle the hassles of life when they are few and far between. When hassles become too frequent they add up to an assault on the mind and body. Elephantine screw-ups get aired and thereby psychologically exorcised. It's the little mosquito bites, too minor to mention—a report that can't be found, forgetting to return a call, failure to perform a little chore—that build up irritation within you and resentment within your boss.

For decades scientists believed that the major crises and changes in our lives caused stress-related disorders. Recent studies have shown little connection between major stresses and illness. There's an old saying that says "(1) Don't sweat the small stuff. (2) It's all small stuff." Before they actually make you ill, how you react to hassles can have a major impact on your career.

Helen, a corporate auditor, had little control over the hot tantrums that consumed her. Ordinary irritations such as traffic jams, silly mistakes, arguments, being given a hard time by a client, having to wait, filling out forms, and so on, irritated her to the point of loud vulgarity.

Helen was reprimanded several times, but she had no control. Slamming doors, yelling, and stomping out of the room became daily occurrences.

When reprimanded her response was, "You sexist pig. If I were a man, you would say I'm assertive. Because I'm a woman you imply I'm a bitch."

Helen was her own worst enemy. She was talented in the technical aspects of her job, but the social necessities escaped her. Plagued by frequent headaches, backaches, and colds, Helen's absentee rate was above the norm.

Helen's supervisor was perplexed. He needed her technical talents but the tantrums had to go. He made the suggestion that she should take a nice, two-week vacation. For once, Helen was agreeable.

Two weeks later Helen returned from a Club Med vacation, with a radiant smile, and plans for an upcoming marriage. Never underestimate love at first sight. Many of us might not pass a second inspection. Suddenly Helen found the little things of life less of a hassle and a new Helen was born. Having someone special helped soften the rough edges in her life. As Jean-Jacques Rousseau said, "Little privations are easily endured when the heart is better treated than the body."

LOVE YOUR WORK

Just as having someone special can help with the burdens of life, so can learning to love your work. If you can't have fun doing your work, if it doesn't fill some of your psychic needs, if you get no satisfaction in your accomplishments at work, perhaps you are in the wrong job or profession. Many people have not discovered their niche, what they really want to do in life. If you are one of these lost souls, this is what you should do:

- Most universities have career centers. Find the one nearest you and make an appointment. These services are usually free or of low cost.
- Tell the career counselor your problem and ask to take a Strong-Campbell Interest Inventory. This inventory can give you great insight into yourself, and will match your interest with occupations that will fill your psychic needs.
- This information may indicate that you will need retraining, a new occupation or profession, and/or that you will need to move on to another company in order to get the kind of job you want. Whatever the cost it will be worth it in the long run. As Confucius said, "Find work that you like to do and you will never have to work again."

MEDITATION

Mediation can help smooth out the rough edges of life. Herbert Benson is the author of *The Relaxation Response* (New York: Avon Books, 1975) and an associate professor at Harvard Medical School. He was doing research on meditation when he was approached by the Transcendental Meditation Organization. They asked him to run a test on their meditators to prove that they could lower their heart rate and relieve hypertension. After the tests were completed, Dr. Benson found that Transcendental Meditation lowered heart rate, blood pressure, the metabolic rate, the rate of oxygen consumption, and also decreased lactic acid in the muscles. Lactic acid is the substance that accumulates in the muscle cells when you experience muscle fatigue and is associated with anxiety.

He also found that meditation has a physiological effect different from sleep or hibernation. You would need four to five hours of sleep to equal the same level of relaxation obtained after just twenty minutes of meditation. That isn't to say you can meditate twice a day and forget about sleep. Meditation is different from sleep and is not a substitute for it. During sleep, oxygen consumption drops 8 percent in four to five hours. During meditation, it drops 10 to 20 percent in three minutes. There's no rapid eye movement found in meditation as there is during sleep.

These findings were publicized by the Transcendental Meditation Organization. When reading this publicity, one is given the impression that TM is uniquely responsible for these results, but Dr. Benson stated that TM is not the only way to elicit the relaxation response. Every culture has its own means of eliciting relaxation: yoga, prayer, chanting, and many other forms of meditation are just as effective. Dr. Benson isolated the different components that allow relaxation to occur during meditation and consequently debunked the mysticism surrounding it. The following is a list of those basic components:

1. Sit quietly in a comfortable position. If you lie down, you may go to sleep. If that is your purpose, then by all means use this technique for inducing sleep. It's a very effective means of turning off the internal dialogues that many times interfere with sleep.
2. Close your eyes. Some forms of meditation have you gaze at a fixed object like a crystal or candle flame. Closing your eyes is much simpler; besides you won't look as weird when you are on an airplane.
3. Say a repeated phrase or word in your mind. Some forms of meditation require that you say the repeated phrase out loud. Again, this practice will make you sound weird on an airplane. The repeated word or phrase can be anything you choose. Dr. Benson says the word "one" is as good as any other. I use "I am" on the inhale and "relaxed" on the exhale, while visualizing the words.

Another myth that Dr. Benson debunked about the TM method was the one about "You must have a special nonsense Sanskrit syllable to repeat that, when repeated, vibrates to your own special vibrations." Only a certified TM teacher knew how to assign you the word, and if you ever told someone your word it wouldn't work anymore. A few years later a TM instructor defected and Parade magazine published how the special words were assigned . . . it was according to your age. My special word at that time was something like "shyhem." I tried it but it didn't do anything for me; but then, I told other people my word.

I once taught a stress management course for a Baptist church. The phrase we used was, "Praise" on the inhale and "Jesus" on the exhale. If you have firm Christian beliefs you may want to try it.

4. Scan your muscles before you begin to make sure that you are not holding any undue muscle tension. Pay particular attention to the lower jaw. Often muscle tension is held there without our awareness. Let your jaw hang loose and slack.

5. Breathe through your nose, not through your mouth. In meditation the metabolism is lowered and so is the need for oxygen. If you breathe through your mouth, you may inhale too much oxygen and become a bit dizzy.

6. Continue repeating your word or phrase for twenty minutes. Any more than twenty minutes and you may go to sleep; any less and your meditation may not get deep enough to give you the full benefit.

7. Do not use an alarm to signal the end of the twenty minutes. Come slowly out of the meditation, give your self a nice stretch, and then just sit there for thirty seconds or so. Most people set an alarm clock for when they want to wake up, yet most people wake up a few minutes before the alarm, if they have had a full night's sleep. It seems that about eight hours of sleep is the natural amount that most of us need. Twenty minutes of meditation seems to be the natural amount of time that most of us need to meditate.

8. Maintain a passive attitude during meditation. Judging how well you're doing during the meditation is counterproductive. If your mind wanders off your repeated phrase, be aware of it and bring your mind back to your meditation. Don't come down on yourself as in, "Damn, I blew it, my mind wandered off my repeated phrase!"

Dr. Benson found that there was a decrease in the number of people who smoked after twenty-one months of meditating. There was also a decrease in the amount of hard liquor and marijuana consumed after twenty-one months of meditating. It was also found that through meditation, hypertension can be relieved. Many doctors feel that some types of hypertension are caused by chronic stress.

As some wise sage said, "If we can develop some way in which a man can doze in public and still keep from making a fool of himself, we have removed one of the big obstacles to human happiness in modern civilization."

If you are a redneck and don't cotton to all this meditation stuff, you might try whittling. Whittling has many of the requirements needed for meditation.

AEROBIC EXERCISE

Aerobic exercise is defined as activity that increases your heart rate and oxygen consumption to an established target level and keeps it there for at least twenty minutes. Examples are swimming, running, brisk walking, rowing, skipping rope, and Jane Fonda tapes. You should choose an exercise that you enjoy; if you choose one that you detest, you will never stick with it. The benefits of this type of exercise go beyond cardiovascular efficiency; it also makes you more capable of coping with swarms of mosquitoes.

Aerobic exercise and meditation have many similarities. The state of mind, if the exercises are done correctly, is virtually the same. In meditation we are to sit quietly in a comfortable position; in aerobics we should exercise quietly and comfortably. In meditation we should close our eyes or gaze passively; in aerobics we just naturally gaze passively. In meditation we repeat a word or phrase; in aerobics we have the rhythm of the exercise. We meditate for twenty minutes; the same minimum requirement goes for aerobics. Before beginning meditation we scan our muscles, before aerobics we scan and stretch our muscles. In meditation we breathe through our

nose; in aerobics we breathe aerobically as opposed to anaer-
obically, which means beyond our ability to provide oxygen to
our bodies. In meditation we have a passive attitude just as
one should have in aerobics. If you don't perform as well as
you wanted, don't come down hard on yourself.

Before beginning an exercise program, always have a physical examination first. (Now you can't sue me if you die of heart
failure.) Start your program by exercising slowly; never push
yourself to exhaustion. Aerobics should be performed at a rate
such that you are never out of breath. You should be able to
carry on a conversation while performing an aerobic exercise.
If you can talk while exercising, you are probably not over-
extending yourself; if you can sing while exercising, you should
probably put forth a little more effort. Twenty minutes of
exercise three times a week is about all you really need. As
you get into better shape you will most likely want to extend
the twenty-minute period to thirty minutes and increase the
frequency from three days a week to every day.

Never push yourself too far; if you do you might injure
yourself, and once injured you might never start exercising
again.

Michael Murphy, founder of the Big Sur Esalen Institute,
and the cosmic cowboy of the Fritz Perils, Sensitivity Training,
Rebirthing, Polarity Therapy, you-study-my-navel-and-I'll-
study-yours school of thought, has been through every psy-
chobabble experience that ever existed. What is he doing now
to keep his head on straight? Running; aerobic running. Take
a lesson from a man who has tried it all, and found what he
considers the best form of mental hygiene.

I started running in 1974 and I have been running ever since.
I found that after five or six years that my mind was drifting
off my running. I was thinking more and more about the mosquito stings I had suffered during the day. My solution was to
stop running and start joggling. Joggling is running and juggling
at the same time. My mind is fully absorbed by the activity;

there's no room for mosquitoes. When this becomes too easy, I'll *add* a ball.

In 1987 I joggled the New York City Marathon. People lined the street seven deep on both sides. When I ran by joggling, wearing my Uncle Sam costume, people cheered and applauded. For four hours, twenty-nine minutes, thirty-four seconds (predicted time 4:30), I had sustained applause. I felt so good after this event that mosquitoes didn't bother me for months; they knew I was impervious. They just went elsewhere to find softer tissue.

LEARN TO PLAY

The end of labor is to gain leisure.

—ARISTOTLE

What did you do last weekend? Did you go to the beach, have a picnic, or go to a movie? Or did you spend your time mowing the lawn, painting the house or catching up on work that you brought home from the office?

The last time I interviewed an up-and-coming yuppie, I asked him what he did during his leisure time. He said he painted his house. I said, "What! You didn't go to the New Orleans Jazz and Heritage Festival?" He said, "No, I had too much to do around the house." With that answer I knew that he would have no trouble fitting in with the oldies (the ones with the stress-related diseases) in upper management.

The American work ethic says we must be doing something productive at all times. When this attitude is carried over into our leisure activities, they can become as stressful as work. A recent survey by the Hilton Hotels Corporation found that 90 percent of Americans spend almost half their weekend time doing chores or working at their jobs. The result is that the weekend break is no break at all. Friday night feels no different from Sunday night, because we have not used our leisure time for leisure.

Some of us turn leisure time activities into work, rather than activities to be enjoyed. A doctor told a hard-driving friend of mine to exercise to reduce her stress level. She chose LSD jogging (Long Slow Distance). After a few months she decided to train for the New York City Marathon. The marathon was only two short months away, so she had to train like a demon. Her training left her more stressed-out than ever. She turned a leisure time activity into a goal-oriented quest.

As Henry Greber said, "Only a person who can live with himself can enjoy the gift of leisure."

Another leisure time mosquito is to spend most of your leisure time with coworkers. Invariably the topic of discussion will get around to that no-good boss or the lowly work assignment. It's best to have a separate set of friends for play.

Friends are important, but many executives do not make the effort to keep the friends they have or to make new friends. The old adage, "It's lonely at the top," is true. It is also true that it's lonely in the middle. Many executives who are good at professional relationships—conversing with a purpose—aren't comfortable with off-duty socializing and making idle small talk. Some are too tired to try to meet new people but most would just rather curl up in front of the television and let Carson do the small talk for them. The result is they don't have many friends to count on when they need emotional support.

Some people try to cram too many leisure activities into one weekend, or try to tour all of Europe in two weeks. By doing this they don't give themselves time to enjoy anything. Leisure time should be planned with time allotted for each activity. A good time to do this is after lunch on Friday. By that time your local paper will have a list of weekend activities. Approach each weekend as a minivacation.

The "Routine" mosquito can really draw some blood. If you

do the same thing every weekend, it may get old. You may burn yourself out on a particular activity. This isn't to say you should give up a thoroughly enjoyed activity just because you are afraid of getting burned-out. If the boys go out bowling every Friday night and you really get a kick out of it, by all means persist. But instead of mowing the lawn every Saturday morning, give yourself a break once in a while. Hire someone to do it or let it go for a week. Try something new, different, and perhaps . . . exciting. Everyone knows you're a whiz at the bowling alley, but can you play handball? Don't rule out an activity because you feel insecure doing it. If you don't know how to snow ski, the beginner's slopes can be just as terrifying as the expert slopes.

A friend and I decided we would do something different, something we had not done since we were children, something that would help us recapture the spirit of play. We went to Woolworth's and each of us bought a bag of marbles. We went to a playground, found a barren area and drew a circle. We played all afternoon and had a great time. When I told my wife about this she thought I had lost all my marbles.

OTHER INSECTICIDES

Even with play and meditation, everyone has a threshold of irritation. Learning to control our responses to these irritations is one of life's great lessons. A few more suggestions are:

- Drink decaffeinated beverages. Caffeine can make you irritable, jumpy, and have bouts of anxiety. Caffeine over-dose can cause sleeplessness and heartbeat irregularities that will scare the willies out of you. Coffee is not the only thing containing caffeine. Some soft drinks, some teas, and chocolate contain caffeine. Some drink it to get the stimulating effects. As one coffee aficionado said, "The

only trouble with Italian coffee is that a week later you're sleepy again."
- Make a "little bummer list." When many problems are closing in at once, write them all down, arrange them in order of importance and cross off a few at the bottom.
- Be more positive. Change the way you view each little bummer. For example: Instead of considering a delayed flight as a major irritation, learn to use the extra time to catch up on some reading, writing, or to make a friend of a likewise stranded passenger.
- Compartmentalize your emotions. Leave the emotions of a particular situation locked within the confines of that situation. None of us has the luxury of doing one thing at a time. It is easy to allow the emotions created by one event to spill over and affect another unrelated event. I once had a boss that was very good at compartmentalizing. He went through a nasty divorce without any of his staff knowing about it. Not until he called us all into his office did we find out that his wife had left him and had taken his children. He was able to seal off the stress and trauma, and not let the divorce affect his work. Compartmentalizing is easier said than done.
- If you can't change the hassle, change your reaction to it; do something to make it more bearable, e.g., learn to laugh:

    A man went to a psychiatrist and said, "Doc, I don't know what's wrong with me. Sometimes I think I'm a Teepee and at other times I think I'm a Wigwam." The doctor said, "Your problem is simple, you're two tents."

CONCLUSION

*Etiquette means behaving yourself a little
better than is absolutely essential.*
                              —WILL CUPPY

IN THIS BOOK I have used humor to explore many delicate
subjects. There are things of deadly seriousness that can only
be safely mentioned under the cover of a joke. Remember,
when you walk down the street what people essentially notice
about you is the flaw. Pay attention to the "little things."

POSTSCRIPT

IN THIS BOOK, I have given you my most bothersome mosquitoes. I would like for this book to be only the beginning. I would like to be able to give you even more insights into the little things that bite us in the business world and in everyday life.

Do you have a bothersome mosquito that I have not covered? Please share them with me. Type up your thoughts and send them to:

> Vernon Crawford
> 3249 DeSoto St.
> New Orleans, LA 70119

Be sure to include your mailing address and telephone number. Should I use your mosquito in my next book, I will contact you for permission. Your reward will be a copy of the new book. If you want confidentiality, names and places will be changed. If you want your name included in the acknowledgments I shall be happy to do so. Thank you for sharing your experiences.

> Best regards,
> Vernon Crawford